LIFE, LITERATURE AND THE ENVIRONMENT: ESSAYS ON TANURE OJAIDE'S WRITING

Edited By

Onookome Okome

and

Obari Gomba

Copyright © 2019 by Cissus World Press, LLC

All rights reserved.

Except in the case of brief quotations included in critical articles or eviews, no portions of this book may be reproduced without written permission from the publisher.

Publisher's information, address:
Cissus World Press, P.O. Box 240865, Milwaukee, WI 53224
www.cissusworldpressbooks.com

ISBN: 978-1-7335872-2-8
First published in the U.S.A by Cissus World Press

First Edition

Library of Congress Cataloging-in-Publication DataLiterature Collections. I. African Studies II. Literary Criticism III. History/Culture

Acknowledgements

Special thanks to the Conveners of the Third Tanure Ojaide International Conference held at the University of Port Harcourt, Rivers State, Nigeria from May 2 to 5, 2018: Professor Onookome Okome of the Department of English and Film Studies, University of Alberta, Edmonton, Canada, and Professor Okiemute Femi Shaka, Dean of the School of Humanities, University of Port Harcourt.

The Editors appreciate the financial contributions of the College of Liberal Arts and Sciences, University of North Carolina at Charlotte through Dean Nancy Gutierrez, and the University of Port Harcourt through Dean Okiemute Femi Shaka. The Editors also appreciate the efforts of Professor Akinwumi Ogundiran, Chair of Africana Studies Department, University of North Carolina at Charlotte, towards involving Tanure Ojaide's home institution in the seminar and conference celebrating his 70th birthday.

Thanks to all the conference participants from the United States, Canada, South Africa, and across universities and other educational institutions in Nigeria. And many thanks go to the local organizing committee chaired by Dr. Obari Gomba for smoothly conducting the conference from which these papers are selected for publication.

We sincerely thank Dr. Dike Okoro, Chair of Humanities Department, Harris Stowe State University, Missouri, USA, and Dr. Enajite Ojaruega of Delta State University, Abraka, for their assistance to the editors.

Table of Contents

Introduction: Tanure Ojaide's Place and Time
Onookome Okome and Obari Gomba

"Trembling in the Balance:" Liminality and *Nationness* in Tanure Ojaide's Poetry *Onyemaechi Udumukwu*

Nostalgia as Aesthetic in Tanure Ojaide's *In the House of Words*
Saeedat B. Aliyu

Environmental Activism and Poetry: Tanure Ojaide's
The Tale of the Harmattan Honoré Missihoun

Udje Aesthetics in Tanure Ojaide's Poetry
Adetayo Alabi

Signs, Significations and Functions: A Semiotic Approach to Tanure Ojaide's *Delta Blues and Home Songs*
Psalms Emeka Chinaka & Okwudiri Anasiudu

Disillusionment and Absurdity in Tanure Ojaide's
Waiting for the Hatching of a Cockerel and *The Beauty I Have Seen*
Mathias Iroro Orhero & Daniel George Udo

The Signification of Spirituality in Selected Short Stories of Tanure Ojaide
Enajite Eseoghene Ojaruega

Poetics of Dissidence: Nigeria's Political Landscape in Tanure Ojaide's
The Activist and *Matters of the Moment Zaynab Ango*

Marxism and Tanure Ojaide's Social Vision
Adama Haruna Idrisu

Identification through Trauma: A Psychoanalytical Interpretation of Five Poems in Ojaide's *Songs of Myself Linda Jummai Mustafa*

A Socio-Stylistic Appraisal of Selected Poems in Tanure Ojaide's *The Eagle's Vision Moshood Zakariyah and Mariam Titilope Gobir*

Environmental Activism: A Quest for Parity in Tanure Ojaide's *The Tale of the Harmattan Edoama Frances Odueme*

Appendix (Citation on Professor Tanure Ojaide, PhD, NNOM)

Introduction: Tanure Ojaide's Place and Time

Onookome Okome and Obari Gomba

Tanure Ojaide is one of Africa's most decorated writers. He has won many prizes and awards such as: Commonwealth Poetry Prize for the African Region, BBC Arts and Africa Poetry Award, Folon-Nichols Award for Excellence in Writing, Nigerian National Merit Award, to name but a few. The accolades are well-deserved by the writer who has published volumes of poetry, collections of short stories, novels, memoirs, and academic texts. His oeuvre has attracted scholarly attention across the world. Interestingly, his tall standing in the canon of Nigerian literature has also led scholars and institutions to organize international conferences in his honour. The conferences have been held three times so far: twice at Delta State University, Abraka; and once at the University of Port Harcourt. The themes have been "Telling the Niger Delta and Beyond" (2005); "Oil and Literature in the Niger Delta" (2008); and "Life, Literature and the Environment" (2018).

Although Ojaide's writing has diverse influences and import (to the extent that his tenor has global appeal and resonance), the oil-rich Niger Delta region of Nigeria has come to occupy a key place in the critical reception of his works. Let us hope that people will not assume that he writes about the Niger Delta only. Why is the Niger Delta so central to his readers? It is because it a very topical subject in the Nigerian literary tradition. In Nigeria, we find a field of conflicts and a collage of narratives across distinct nationalities and identities of which the Niger Delta has provoked the most incidental literary harvests of the last thirty years.

The Niger Delta is a veritable site of narratives. The ethnic groups in the region have a strong sense of attachment to territory, as an amalgam of ethnic groups in a plural society. They are the kind of ethnic groups that Haralambos and Holborn have defined as "culturally distinctive within 'colonially created'" nation-states (159); they are groups that constitute a region of "aboriginal inhabitants" who see themselves as "politically relatively powerless" and "partially integrated into the dominant [stream of the] nation-state" (159). The strategies of empowerment which these disparate units have adopted are conflictual today as they were in the past. Of course, this has been the feature of many postcolonial societies. There is always conflict in polities where colonialism has yoked disparate peoples in nation-states. There has been an escalation of conflict in many of such societies in recent times, and this has proved that the assumptions of Western hegemony, concerning the nation-states, have been wrong.

As Haralambos and Holborn have noted, most theories of the West "assumed that the nineteenth century saw the successful establishment of distinct nations and that regional differences within nation-states would tend to disappear as time progressed" (191). Haralambos and Holborn also note that Stuart Hall has observed that "both of 'the discourse of modernity,'" namely liberalism and Marxism, "led people 'to expect not the revival but the gradual disappearance of the nationalist passion'" (188). On one hand, Marxist theory held that "classes, not nations, would become the great historical actors;" on the other hand, "liberalism saw national difference being eroded by a global market in which trade linked all parts of the world" (Haralambos and Holborn 188). These assumptions have not materialized in the reality of many postcolonial nation-states. In fact, the Niger Delta example shows that the issues of accumulation and distribution have stoked the fire of nationalism in nation-states. And nationalism has given rise to violent resistance in many places where change has not been negotiated with ease.

Given the nationalistic rage-and-fire in the Niger Delta, people are poised to right the wrongs of history and to upturn the perceived vestiges of colonization. This kind of agitation has mostly confirmed that "decolonization is always a violent phenomenon" (Fanon 27). We can turn to Hannah Arendt for a clear perspective on the upsurge of violence as a natural reaction which is provoked by obduracy: "Rage is by no means an automatic reaction to misery and suffering" (in Watts 101). Arendt also says that "Only where there is reason to suspect that conditions could be changed and are not does rage arise. Only when one's sense of justice is offended do we react with rage;" and to "resort to violence when confronted with outrageous events or conditions is enormously tempting because of its inherent immediacy and swiftness" (in Watts 101). She adds that "under certain circumstances, violence – acting without counting the consequences – is the only way to set the scales of justice right again" (in Watts 101). This observation has been true of many postcolonial societies. The nation-states that have been fashioned by colonialism have proved to be sure sites of obduracy. Those nation-states make it difficult for the constituent units to negotiate change, and (as we see in Ojaide's writing) the situation leads to the catharsis of violence and revolt against existing orders of state.

Every nation-state has those who profit from the status quo and the profiteers exist by the calcified habits of repression. The profiteers create hegemony and bump into the sentimentality and/or actuality of nationalism which is nursed by the disadvantaged units of the nation-state. When new orders of nationality begin to stir awake among the repressed, they latch onto their pain as the flint of solidarity, and the fire of resistance is ignited in the soul of the nation(s).

Ernest Renan is right when he says a "nation is a soul, a spiritual principle.... A nation is... a large scale solidarity," which is hinged on historic perceptions of bonding, "constituted by the feeling of the sacrifices that one has made in the past and of those that one is prepared to make in the future" (19). Of course this soul "presupposes a past" but "it is summarized, however, in the present by a tangible fact, namely consent, the clearly expressed desire to continue a common life" (Renan 19). Such a solidarity or uprising is never without its faultlines and ambivalences; it also never fails to mark the poles of conflict on the binary of We/Us and They/Them. Thus, it never fails to generate narratives because the calibrations of history become the tremors of nations: their "beingness," their bonds and conflicts, their success and failures are the sources for narratives such as Ojaide's.

We see in Ojaide's oeuvre that "narration" and "nation" are inextricable. In sync with Homi Bhabha's idea of "DissemiNation," Ojaide's writing on the Niger Delta shows how the souls of the minority nations have been stirred by the incongruities of their postcoloniality. The meat of this "DissemiNation" is in the last six letters which foreground "Nation" and the capacity of a *nation* to provoke narratives by its pains and by its resistance against hegemony. The stories of the Niger Delta nationalities follow this pattern. The narratives of Ojaide's writing constitute literary "DissemiNation" on/of pain and resistance, with all the shades in between. Ojaide uses the tropes of art to represent what Bhabha calls "the discourse of minorities" (245). A key aspect of this discourse is hinged on resource-extraction and environmental despoliation.

For example, there is the enunciation of oil and conflict in Ojaide's *The Activist* and in many of his poems. The manner of depiction shows a continuum of repression and resistance in the Niger Delta. The depiction reaches the core of postcolonial concerns because the works indicate how the postcolonial turn has been conditioned by the experience of colonialism. Ojaide qualifies to be read as a postcolonial writer by all standards. His writing comes under the timespan of postcolonial experience, not just in terms of the period of authorship and publication, but in terms of its socio-political and cultural concerns.

For the avoidance of doubt, oil is at the root of the fortunes and/or misfortunes of Nigeria's postcolonial experience. Oil is the basic motivation for the tremors of agitation in the Niger Delta, and the agitation stems from the feeling of discontent against Nigeria's postcolonial order. The oil-bearing nationalities have come to see Nigeria as extended colonialism, and this feeling of discontent is seen in Ojaide's writing. By reading Ojaide's works, attention is called to the ethnic question in Nigeria. Rather than class dialectics, ethnicity is the hinge for the discontent of oil-bearing nationalities; that is what Ken Saro-Wiwa calls "the ethnic question and oil" (63). Class dialectics tends to mask the ethnic import of oil-conflict in postcolonial Nigeria. Unlike class dialectics, Bhabha's "DissemiNation" fits the mode of Ojaide's writing because it enables us to see the narratives of the minorities as the positions of nations and as the interrogation of old orders of nationality by new or persisting realities. In a similar context, Saro-Wiwa has averred that "the ethnic nature of Nigerian society is a real one," and he draws largely from the insight of Obafemi Awolowo whom he credits for querying the nature of the Nigerian state. Awolowo is quoted to have noted that under "a true Federal constitution, each group, however small is entitled to the same treatment as any other group, however large," small nations deserve a foothold in the polity, and "opportunity must be afforded to each to evolve its own peculiar political institution. The present structure of Nigeria reinforces indigenous colonialism – crude, harsh, unscientific and illogical system" (Saro-Wiwa 63). It is the failure to guarantee the rights of the ethnic minorities (to their resource and environment) that has provoked images in Ojaide's writing.

Whereas this writing strongly points to how the ethnic question has continued to mark the daily experiences of Niger Delta peoples / Nigerians, literary scholars sometimes tend to either ignore or skim over the pointers to the situation. More can be done in postcolonial interpretations of Nigerian (and African) literature to examine the structure of relationships between the component units of previously colonized peoples, to examine the emergence of centres and margins within the borders of the nation-states that have been fashioned by imperial Europe, to examine how today's inequalities stand on the plinth of colonial past and on the props of present Western interest, to examine the on-going waves of resistance and the clamour for self-determination (by marginalized units) which give veracity to what Awolowo calls indigenous colonialism. These issues are at the root of most upheavals in postcolonial states. They are specifically at the root of the resource conflict in the Niger Delta. Martin Meredith has noted that "the main grievance of [Niger] Delta activists [is] that oil revenue produced by the [Niger] Delta [is] used largely to benefit ethnic majority areas of the country" while the peoples of the [Niger] Delta "suffer from neglect" (576).

It is clear that Meredith, Awolowo and Saro-Wiwa have raised a point that is crucial to our understanding of oil and conflict in Ojaide's writing. This can help us to locate Ojaide's writing within the provisions of postcolonial theory, and it can reveal how postcolonial theory interlaces the poetics of social function. It shows how the paradigms of repression and resistance play out in his writing. It shows that oil-provoked conflicts stem primarily from the actions and reactions of nations and/or from the agitations of nations that are trapped in the suzerainty of nation-states. It shows Ojaide's commitment to narrating the margins of the Nigerian state: the tenor of the works has historicised and periodized experiences, and it keeps the nations at the centre of representation.

Ojaide's carries his mantle properly. Biodun Jeyifo, in a different context, has described that mantle as the "tradition of the Third World writer as a promoter of explicit social, political, and moral values crucial to the survival of his or her society and [as] a champion of freedom, dignity, and justices" (ix). In the opening chapter of *Ordering*, simply entitled "The Challenges of the African Writer Today," Ojaide says "[a] writer is not an air plant but the product of a specific place and time, which have their cultural, social, economic and political manifestations"(1). Ojaide says a writer "is intricately bound to the destiny of the place and time" that has "nurtured him or her. The problems of the writer's place or environment and period are therefore the writer's own problems too" (1). Ojaide says that "the challenges of the writer in Africa today are, to a large extent, the challenges of his or her own African peoples arising from their being Africans in this era and by virtue of the environment" (1).

Ojaide further narrows the subject down in the third chapter of *Ordering* (entitled "Nativity and the Creative Process: The Niger Delta in my Poetry"). He avers that "there is an accumulation of forces deriving from the particular nature and condition" of his Niger Delta nativity (37). He notes that the Niger Delta "is a body of place and a spirit" (37). "I am not an air plant," he says, "I may travel the world and live elsewhere but I am physically and psychically anchored to the Niger Delta. It is the driving spirit of the [Niger] Delta that shapes the vision and provides the images in my writing" (37). He is a writer who has a strong sense of place and commitment. He understands that the Niger Delta is indeed one of the hottest sites of conflict. His Niger Delta nativity bears the marks of the history of colonialism as it concerns the issues of oil resources in Nigeria's postcolonial scheme. He knows that the inhabitants of the Niger Delta are minority-nationalities within the Nigerian federation. The country has a grip on all resources in the Niger Delta, and "the status of these minorities is," as he notes, "that of…exploited people(s)" (36). This, for him, is the reason why "the [Niger] Delta writer's orientation is to signify the [Niger] Delta, showing its paradox of sitting on oil and yet remaining impoverished" (36). He knows that a sense of nativity has stoked the conflict of interest between the exploited minorities and "the majority-dominated Nigerian polity," to the point that minority-peoples have "moved…to political agitation against exploitation" (37).

His creative oeuvre offers some of the highly perceptive images that can enable us examine a wide range of the Niger Delta's experience and a great deal of the human condition. For this reason, Onyemaechi Udumukwu, Seedat Aliyu, Honore Missihuon, Adetayo Alabi, Psalms Chinaka, Okwudiri Anasiudu, Mathias Orhero, Daniel George Udo, Enajite Ojaruega, and Zaynab Ango have contributed essays to explicate the manner and matter of Ojaide's writing. Some of the essays discuss the Niger Delta beyond oil and strife; and by that, they extend the scope of Ojaide's place and time.

Udumukwu's "'Trembling in the Balance:' Liminality and *Nationness* in Tanure Ojaide's Poetry," a keynote at the third international conference on Ojaide, examines the Niger Delta as a population at the "in-between space" of the Nigerian state. To reveal Ojaide's depiction of "liminality," Udumukwu cites poems from Ojaide's *The Endless Song, The Fate of Vultures and Other Poems*, and *The Blood of Peace and Other Poems* to buttress his point. Aliyu's essay, "Nostalgia as Aesthetic in Tanure Ojaide's *In the House of Words*," discusses the aesthetic value of reminiscence in Ojaide's poetry. The capacity of the poet-persona - to remember the past, "imagine" the present, and project into the future - positions the poems as sites of deep experience that are filled with socio-political implications. Missihoun's "Environmental Activism and Poetry: Tanure Ojaide's *The Tale of the Harmattan*" looks at Ojaide's depiction of the environmental degradation of the Niger Delta. He sees resource extraction and the politics of control as related problems in the region, and he argues that Ojaide's confronts the problems by creating insightful images.

Alabi writes, in "Udje Aesthetics in Tanure Ojaide's Poetry," that Ojaide's poetry draws from the oral resources of the Urhobo people of the Niger Delta. To illustrate Ojaide's craft, the essay has cited two of Ojaide's books entitled *Poetry, Performance, and Art: Udje Dance Songs of the Urhobo People* (a text of literary criticism) and *Songs of Myself: Quartet* (a collection of poems). This implies that Alabi has hinged his interpretation of the latter on Ojaide's postulations in the former.

Chinaka and Anasiudu have, in "Signs, Significations and Functions: A Semiotic Approach to Tanure Ojaide's *Delta Blues and Home Songs*," critiqued one of Ojaide's most popular poetry collections. For a collection of this significance, they have brought freshness to their exegesis through a linguistic interpretation of the poems. Orhero and Udo argue that there is "Disillusionment and Absurdity in Tanure Ojaide's *Waiting for the Hatching of a Cockerel* and *The Beauty I Have Seen*" and they proceed to interpret Ojaide's vision and activism by using the theory of existentialism. They state that they have selected both collections because the texts represent a crucial landmark in Ojaide's artistic imagination.

Ojaruega and Ango have written about Ojaide's fiction. Ojaruega's "The Signification of Spirituality in Selected Short Stories of Tanure Ojaide" examines the writer's portrayal of spirituality in some short stories selected from three of Ojaide's collections: *God's Medicine-Men and Other Stories, The Debt-Collector and Other Stories* and *The Old Man in a State House and Other Stories*. Whereas Ojaruega explicates Ojaide's short stories, Ango discusses two novels in her essay, "Poetics of Dissidence: Nigeria's Political Landscape in Tanure Ojaide's *The Activist* and *Matters of the Moment*." Ango uses Michel Foucault's theorization of power and resistance to explain why rebellion is a fundamental recourse of a subjugated society. She argues that Ojaide presents rebellion as the most viable line of action open to the masses in the face of repression.

The essays in this book are very important because they are earnest discussions on the writing of an outstanding writer. They do not in any way exhaust the perspectives on his writing. Neither do they discuss all his works. But anyone who is going to study his works henceforth will not ignore what has been said about him here. Let us note that those future scholars do not have to agree with everything that has been said here. We expect that every new reading of the author will give rise to new ways of knowing him.

Works Cited

Bhabha, Homi K. *The Location of Culture*. Routledge, 1994.

Fanon, Frantz. *The Wretched of the Earth*. Penguin, 1967.

Haralambos, Michael, and Martin Holborn.
Sociolgy: Themes and Perspectives. 7th ed. HarperCollins, 2008.

Jeyifo, Biodun. "Mythopoeisis and Commitment". Introduction.
Wole Soyinka: An Introduction to His Writing. By Obi Maduakor.
Heinemann, 1987. ix-xv.

Meredith, Martin. *The Fate of Africa:
A History of Fifty Years of Independence*. Public Affairs, 2005.

Ojaide, Tanure. *Ordering the African Imagination:
Essays on Culture and Literature*. Malthouse, 2007.

Renan, Ernest. "What is a Nation?" *Nation and Narration*. Ed. Homi K. Bhabha. Routledge, 1990. 8-22.

Saro-Wiwa, Ken. *A Month and a Day: A Detention Diary*. Safari Books, 1995.

Watts, Michael ."Sweet and Sour". *Curse of the Black Gold: 50 Years of Oil in the Niger Delta*. Ed. Michael Watts. PowerHouse Books, 2008. 36-47.

"Trembling in the Balance:"
Liminality and *Nationness* in Tanure Ojaide's Poetry

Onyemaechi Udumukwu

Introduction

In his earlier study on the poetry of Tanure Ojaide, Terhemba Shija asserts that "Ojaide explores the bourgeois society with the eyes of a common man" (32). Implicit in this assertion is the hinge point for our own account on the background of Ojaide's poetry. This underscores the ambivalence of the nation manifesting in the two realities, subject conditions, and centers of consciousness in Shija's assertion. Metonymy and synecdoche are important tropes in Shija's expression above. By "bourgeois society," he refers to the political and economic elite that inherited the mantle of leadership in postcolonial Nigeria.

Political economists have explained the emergence of this class of leadership. Speaking against the background of his account on the postcolonial, Claude Ake had argued that the *post* in "postcolonial," especially as used in the sub-Saharan African context, evokes a sense of ambiguity. This is because the term "postcolonial" especially in the context of sub-Saharan Africa does not mean that "an economy has been decolonized and no longer possesses features of a colonial economy" (88). The symptom of this negation, Ake has shown, is the prevalence of "enclave development" especially in the sense that development activities and the provision of social amenities are concentrated in a few centres. Ake blames this situation on the emergent petty-bourgeois class that took over from the colonialists. He asserts that members of this class were interested in inheritance. It is this kind of inheritance that defines what Shija calls "bourgeois society". But observe that as Shija tells us, Ojaide is not entrapped by this kind of society and its imaginary. Rather he explores it, interrogating its imaginary through "the eyes of the common man." Achille Mbembe has explained that the emergence of these two centers of consciousness is indicative of "the privatization of public prerogative and the socialization of arbitrariness ... which became the cement of postcolonial African regimes" (32). Observe that private and public choices are standing side-by-side with the socialization or communalization of arbitrariness. This will become clearer in the course of this study.

It means, therefore, that the inherited structure, called "bourgeois society" has created a form that sets it side-by-side with another, in fact its *other*, the common man. Observe also that we are told that Ojaide relates to this society with the "eyes of the common man." By the "eyes of the common man," Shija underscores a new subjectivity. This is a subjectivity that is capable of seeing and of perception. In other words, postcolonial Nigeria is a world torn into two; it is a Manichean world of a petty-bourgeois group and a world populated by the "common man." Our account will negotiate both the political and ideological contexts of these two worlds and the literary response emanating from them. In fact, Ojaide's poetry is permeated by an internal opposition between two centers of consciousness, manifesting in a "we-they" kind of relationship. It is a relationship that neither ends in a dialogical unity, a condition of harmony between opposites nor is resolved in a state of nihilism and despondency. Rather the speaking voice in each poem envisions the hope that a new order will emerge out of the fusion of the opposites. In the course of this discussion, we will see how the clash between these two worlds has engendered the poetry of Ojaide.

We need to explain a key term in our title, *"nationness."* Homi Bhabha used the word in his introduction to *Nation and Narration.* Thus, he notes that the nation is "constituted from competing dispositions of human association as *societas* (the acknowledgement of moral rules and conventions of conduct) and *universitas* (the acknowledgment of common purpose and substantive end). In other words, the nation, understood as an "imagined political community…and imagined as both inherently limited and sovereign" (Anderson 6), is not a fixed totality. Rather it is an ideal that we realize in practice, in the activities of actual men and women who are products of different *societas.* Members of a given *societas* relate to the "imagined community" on the basis of identified interest. But often the different interests will clash, thereby putting to question our entrance into the imagined community. Our use of *nationness* is also symptomatic of the immanent contradictions, the uneven distribution of wealth and infrastructure, the pain that results thereof. These are all the lubricating factors on our way to the ideal imagined community. We share Bhabha's optimism on the potential of narrative and literature in general to illuminate the inherent ambivalence. It is this kind of optimism that has motivated our own study on Ojaide's poetry within the context of postcolonial Nigeria.

Even though the term postcolonial continues to be controversial and contentious, it is important to apprehend our use of the term and its intersection with Ojaide's poetry. The controversy is hinged on whether "postcolonial" refers to after colonial rule especially as is suggested in the prefix, *post*, or whether we should agree with Bill Ashcroft, Gareth Griffiths and Helen Tiffin that "postcolonial" should mean rooted from the onset of colonial rule. According to Ashcroft, Griffiths and Tiffin: "We use the term 'postcolonial' to cover all the cultures affected by the imperial process from the moment of colonization to the present day" (2). In addition, they explain: "this is because there is continuity of preoccupations throughout the historical process initiated by European imperial aggression" (2).

Ania Loomba subtly agrees with the foregoing conception of "postcolonial." She reasons thus: "if the inequities of colonial rule have not been erased, it is perhaps premature to proclaim the demise of colonialism" (7). In other words, even though formal direct colonialism is over, the former colonized nations and people are still under colonization. The key word in Loomba's reasoning is "demise" connecting to the prefix, "post" in postcolonial. What this portends is that since the "inequities of colonialism" are still active then colonialism itself is not over. Ashcroft, Griffiths and Tiffin have modified the earlier view in their later work, *Post-Colonial Studies: The Key Concepts*. Thus, we are told that "post-colonialism deals with the effects of colonization on cultures and societies" (186). If indeed we view postcolonialism in terms of the continued effects of colonialism and construe those effects as the iniquities of European colonization, it is important to underscore that colonialism, like all historical events, produced effects; but it also produced a historical sense. We think that what has become pertinent at the end of the nationalist struggle is what African nations have done with that particular historical sense that emerged from European colonialism. Achille Mbembe is of the view that African political elite had indiscriminately adopted the practices of the colonizers and so have created a situation of extreme material scarcity, uncertainty and inertia"(24). He explains, in addition, that "the colonial rationality...were [sic] quickly re-appropriated by Africans. This re-appropriation was not merely institutional; it also occurred in material spheres and in the spheres of the imaginary" (40). Even though Mbembe has provided elaborate examples of the manifestations of the process of re-appropriation in sub-Saharan Africa, we think that the Nigerian situation may prove that adoption of colonial practices was quite inventive and contrary to the earlier view by Loomba. The appropriation of colonial legacy did not happen automatically but followed a deliberate though selfish manipulation of a historical sense.

The significance of the foregoing account on indirect rule and its pattern of appropriation in postcolonial Nigeria is that the theme of the conference on Ojaide is "Literature, Life and the Environment." In explaining this theme in relation to our discussion, we will recall the assertion made by the French writer Stendhal, that literature is like a gunshot in the middle of a concert. It is something malevolent which no one can ignore. Indeed following from this, Ojaide's poetry, especially in its second phase of development, has become that veritable gunshot in the middle of our political life. But critics and students of Ojaide's poetry have been carried away by the reflection of the physical environment because that is what we easily see. We tend to have forgotten that the images of decay and the devastation are mere symptoms on the surface.

This mandates that we explain Ojaide's poetry by understanding the underlying politics that have engendered it and how that politics have produced a particular environment. Mamdani has identified this "politics" as the "postcolonial dilemmas" (657-661), especially the complicated nature and contradictions in the redefinition of the divide between indigene and settler and how the crisis therein both affect and is the basis for exploiting the environment.

Ojaide's creativity may have been animated by a kind of politics but he is also a bearer of a poetic tradition. We use "bearer" here in that unique sense in which T.S. Eliot has described the relationship between the poet and his tradition. According to Eliot, "no poet, no artist of any art, has his complete meaning alone. His significance, his appreciation is the appreciation of his relation to the *dead poets and artists*" (Eliot 1093). Ojaide's relation extends not only to the dead poets of Africa but equally to the living. Ultimately, he is incomplete without the forces that have shaped modern African poetry. Therefore, we will describe briefly, the nature of this poetic tradition of which he has both followed and reshaped.

In the conclusion to his contribution on the task of domesticating modern African poetry, D.I. Nwoga argues that: "Domesticated African poetry.... is that which talks to as many Africans as possible about issues of greatest relevance in Africa's ongoing development" (53). Nwoga's vision is that of a tradition of poetry that has a general appeal, especially in terms of readership and relevance. Furthermore, he avers that "it is poetry which is not a repetition of the past, but is adequate for today because, though based on the past, it is using all the techniques offered by a wider world to cope with the sensibilities generated by Africa's history" (53).

The significance of Nwoga's contribution is that he underscores that delicate link with the past. It is a link that is not a mere repetition but a synthesis in such a way that is adequate for the needs of today. Shija has identified this synthetic sensibility as the key feature of Ojaide and his contemporaries. This sensibility, according to Shija, manifests in "the adoption of elements of the oral tradition" (27). Ojaide, he further argues, "belongs to the third generation of modern African poetry." Members of this generation share some features in common namely,

Their eclectic style manifesting in the free borrowing of techniques from the older generation of poets and from the oral tradition.

The poets of Ojaide's generation adopt a "populist approach towards poetry" (29). Thus the medium of dissemination of poetry has been democratized to involve "all media of mass communication" (29).

The influence from the Association of Nigeria Authors (ANA). As Shija has observed, this association organizes poetry reading sessions at university campuses and cities across the nation. The association has instituted annual poetry prizes that attract new writers. Apart from the ANA prize, it is equally important to recall the role of other literary prizes.

Shija also recalls the perceptive view of Tijan Sallah (16) on the contribution of poets of Ojaide's generation. Thus:

These poets have assumed the task of art for social advocacy in the hope of quickening the possibility of attainment of a better world.

They have employed their art to engineer purposeful social change.

They employ the magical potency of language in order to radically alter the landscape of complacent minds and inspire them to fashion a more humane future.

There are key issues to be picked up from this assertion which are pertinent to our understanding of the poetry of Ojaide. These key points are as follows:

Poetry is an art for both social advocacy and for the attainment of a better world. It reminds us of a key assertion by Karl Marx that philosophers have interpreted the world in so many ways but the overall task is to change it. And as we noted earlier in our discussion, the Nigerian state turned the Nigerian world upside down at independence but it could not change it. Ojaide's poetry is committed to this inevitable change

The foregoing is connected to the second point in Sallah's claim that the new generation of poets "employed their art to engineer purposeful social change".

The third issue is the role and power of language in the hands of this generation of poets. Sallah refers to the magical potency of language, its connotative density and even clarity that yields it to "alter the landscape of the complacent minds and inspire them to fashion a humane future." This is significant because it underscores the power of words as weapons of social change. Words can reshape our thought pattern by reengineering our mindsets and shocking us out of our condition of ignorance. There is even a more urgent political relevance of this assertion. We are living in a world where a certain kind of political change has, in reality, turned our lives and our world upside down. But the real need is to change it. This can be done when we allow language, as we see in the poetry of Ojaide, to reorder our values, our orientation, and shake us away from the pit of complacency to action.

The consequence of the growing tendency of indigeneity as a test for rights in postcolonial Nigeria underwrites the very relationship between literary production, life and the environment. This is because indigeneity has not only defined life in Nigeria but it is at the foundation of the destruction of the environment in the Niger Delta. It animates and fuels the commodification of the physical environment manifesting in the oil and gas explorations and expropriation in the Niger Delta region. It is equally responsible for the indifferent and elusive response to the waves of internal displacement in the region. Ojaide's poetry, therefore, engages these crises of indigeneity by illuminating the pain of the victims who, though indigenes, are either displaced or abandoned in the in-between space of nationhood. Our focus in this study is on what Onookome Okome has described as the second phase in the development of Ojaide's poetry. This phase is focused on the destruction of the ecosystem, the desecration of the divinity, the disillusionment of the people and the neglect of the Niger Delta (Okome cited in Shija, 85). Unlike the universalist and abstract concern of the first phase or the trans-nationalist and diasporic preoccupation of the third phase, the second phase is focused on the issues of *nation-ness*, and national becoming.

Liminality

The word liminality (noun) is derived from two other related words, "limen" (noun) and "liminal" (adjective). According to *The New Webster's Dictionary of the English Language*, "limen" is derived from psychology and means the threshold of consciousness, the limit below which a stimulus is not perceived. Its etymological root is the Latin word, *liminis*, meaning threshold. The adjective "liminal" is also common in psychology and used in relation to or pertaining to the limen or threshold. Lee Rozelle has shown that the liminal is conception that traditionally finds relevance in both psychology and anthropology. According to Rozelle, modern conceptions of liminality can be found in Arnold van Gennep's *The Rites of Passage* and later developed by anthropologist Victor Turner. For both van Gennep and Turner, initiates in rites of passage must go through three basic stages: separation, limen, and reincorporation. Turner, Rozelle further explains, goes on to describe the liminal as "interval, however brief, of margin or limen, when the past is momentarily negated, suspended, or abrogated and the future has not yet begun. It is an instance of pure potentiality when everything as it were, 'trembles in the balance'" (Rozelle 444).

An important aspect of the concept of liminality and its associated terms, limen and luminal, is the sense of the interstitial or the in-between space, a threshold area that sets the term apart from the more definite word, limit. It is also this aspect of the interstitial that has been appropriated by postcolonial theory in order to account for the consequence of the effect of transition from the colonial context and the potentiality in the new order after colonialism. Bill Ashcroft, Gareth Griffiths and Helen Tiffin explain that "the colonized subject may dwell in the liminal space between colonial discourse and the assumption of the new 'non-colonial identity'" (130). In other words, within the colonial discourse, as in the earlier uses of the concept of liminality in anthropology, the idea of transition is consistent. However, they caution that such transition is not automatic or a simple movement from one identity, say colonial or native, to another, say non-colonized. Rather they underscore that the transition occurs on the basis of the process of appropriation, of engagement and interrogation. Accordingly, you may be a native, an indigene, but still be trapped in the in-between space between colonialism and independence, between the past and the present. Even though the individual is no longer in the past, because colonialism is over, he has not begun to fully live the present; this is because the legacy of colonialism shuts him or her out of the gains of independence.

This recalls the account of Homi Bhabha in *The Location of Culture*. Bhabha quotes the art historian, Renee Green, in his description of a staircase as a "liminal space, a parting between upper and lower areas, each of which was annotated with plaques referring to racial differences of blackness and whiteness" (Bhabha 4). The significance of this is that liminality is not just the space of appropriation but it is a threshold of "unhappy consciousness" and therefore, of change. If we recall Martin Heidegger's idea that "space is a mode of one's existence in the world" (Gelven 67), what Ojaide has seen and continues to see is a mode of existence in the nation-space from the limen, in-between reality of the past and the present. And it is this kind of "in-betweenness" that interrogates the sense of African history as "collective experience."

Liminality as Space of Appropriation

The idea of the liminal as a space of appropriation, of engagement, and of contestation is vividly but rhetorically represented in the poem, "The vision," which is published in the collection, *The Endless Song*. "The vision" is a poem of twenty four lines and six sentences. The speaking voice begins by expressing an awareness of experience in the liminal space. He announces a relationship between "us" and a dominant figure or subject, "the leopard." The relationship between "us" and this dominant subject manifests in the reality of "us" as the haunted. In haunting "us," the dominant subject has created a space of closure, but a closure tantamount to its own inauthenticity. It is that space of closure that provokes the sense of engagement and of appropriation. Thus the persona declares out of his condition of "haunt" that the "leopard will die" (l.1). Observe that "haunt" connotes the following: trouble, tribulation, difficulty, breakdown, woe, and anxiety. These connotations convey a situation that is opposed to desire but rather than succumbing to despair, the persona is defiant. It is this willpower that has animated the declaration: "leopard will die." This is a declaration of both possibility and of authenticity and it confirms the liminal space as the space of becoming, of opportunity, as a passage to a new beginning.

The poem follows an epigram from Otto Rene Castillo that asserts: "Beneath our night / a sun awaits us" (2). Two realities are juxtaposed in this assertion, night and sun, despair and hope. Observe also, the references to space in this poem. These include: "ambush," "hearth," "dump," "outside," "the bush," "the road," and "the earth." The significance of these references to space is that they serve to mark the idea of the in-between. Take for example "road" which expresses the idea of linkage between points. "Ambush" is both a verb and a noun and it conveys the sense of trap and ensnare; and that of surprise. It also suggests its opposite, freedom. With this realization of possibility, the persona equally expresses the need for appropriation and engagement. Between lines 16 – 22, he underscores the need for engagement thus:

> It is not the habit of the hunter
> to blind himself with drinks, no,
> he must have a clear vision of the game,
> then listen to movement, breath and smell-
> silence is his guide.
> He knows where to hit the big game once,
> Just once, and it falls.

The parable of the hunter is indicative of the qualification for appropriation and engagement that are basic in the liminal space. The fundamental issue is that of clear-sightedness, acute sense of judgement on the immanent opportunity and possibility at the threshold. In short, liminality is a place of transition, a journey through the wilderness of nationhood.

Read within the liminal space of the Niger Delta, "The vision" is a call to arms, a call to militant resistance. This call becomes imperative because as the persona underscores: "let us not dance because we won the mock-battle" (l.4). The "mock battle" resonates all past struggles and victories, including independence and even past agitations for political units and participations. The story of the Niger Delta from the time of colonialism through the anti-colonial struggle and postcolonial era testifies that the region has only witnessed "mock battles" that have ended as reactionary responses and momentary victories. It is against this kind of atrocious and abhorrent space that the persona in "The vision" cries out:

> We have to incur debts to buy new weapons
> or mend our broken ones,
> then go to the bush to prove our mettle.. (ll 8-10)

The key point here is the call to appropriation and the need to recreate the woes associated with our liminal space in the Niger Delta.

The ideas of appropriation and engagement resonate acutely in the poem, "We Keep Watch over Them," also published in *The Endless Song*. The poem is arranged in forty-one lines and in six stanzas. Although there is no uniform order in the arrangement of the lines but it is intriguing to observe that the first stanza has four lines, the second has six lines; the third has eight lines while the fourth and fifth have seven lines. The last stanza has nine lines. Although it is important to note this irregular pattern of arrangement, it is equally important to note that the irregularity contributes to the overarching meaning of unhappy consciousness in the poem. To recall Bhabha, the stanzas, in their irregularity, are like "annotated plaques" of experience in the liminal space of the Niger Delta. While the "annotated plaques" in Renee Green's picture represent two racial experiences, of blackness and whiteness, the irregular shaped plaques in Ojaide's poem capture the experience of pain, savagery and the metal will to combat. The sombre tone soon explodes in a militant frenzy precipitated by the horrid pain. Thus the persona screams in the first stanza:

From the scaffold of pain we keep watch over them,
from the perilous precipice of misery we keep watch over them,
from the exposed post of lowliness, cold and clammy,
from the slums of existence we keep watch over them (ll. 1-4)

Observe the pervading effect of the liminal space in these lines. The shapes of space are strung like those annotated plaques we referred to earlier but they stand out here in their grim images as "the scaffold of pain," "the perilous precipice of misery," "the post of lowliness," and "the slums of existence." Recall also Heidegger's idea of space as the mode of one's existence. When we read these lines, they are evocative of the outposts in the waterside communities in the Niger Delta, with their shacks on stilts. Note the lives of the inhabitants of these outposts are on stilts, on makeshifts, and not yet at their limits. But the persona characterizes these outposts as the domain of pain, peril, and misery. This perilous asymmetry is provoked by the culture of tyranny and violence captured from the second stanza. Thus:

When they savage us, we withdraw to cabal;
our experience over the ages helps us through
our women know how to march naked at twilight
and rid the land of tormentors,
our men know how to bury despots with their paraphernalia...

The question may be asked whether there is a difference between "tyranny" and "violence." Tyranny manifests in Ojaide's poem as the despotic rule and unjust and cruel exercise of power. Ordinarily, violence means the use of physical force so as to damage. Within the context of anti-colonial consciousness and post-colonial theory, it simply means "outrage" especially against sources and forces of tyranny and injustice. According to Mamdani, this kind of violence is the "midwife of history" (1). It is, he argues, "the kind of violence that turns "victims into killers" (5). It is "the violence of yesterday's victims, the violence of those who had cast aside their victimhood to become masters of their own lives" (5). This is violence that is rooted in Frantz Fanon's paean of anti-colonialism, *The Wretched of the Earth*.

The distinction between "tyranny" and "violence" which we have tried to establish here has become necessary because there is a current literature on Ojaide's poetry that amounts to a misreading of his use of violence. In the lines above, from *The Endless Song*, the reference to tyranny is introduced in the words, "they" and "savage." Let us examine "savage" first. *The New Webster's Dictionary of the English Language* has two main entries for the word "savage." First is as an adjective, in which it means primitive, uncivilized; characteristic of a primitive and uncivilized people or wild and ferocious and extremely cruel. The second is as a noun, meaning uncivilized human being, especially one who is cruel and uncultivated. There is a third but minor use of the word as a transitive verb, as in savaging. In this usage, it means to attack, bite, claw, and rend. Ojaide's use of the word "savage" is rooted in this minor significance but he removes it from its minor value and underscores it in relation to tyranny and power.

Now, lets us get back to the word, "they." The persona introduces a "they"-"us" relationship in line 5. Who are the "they"? "They" are the "tormentors" in line 8 and the "despots" in line 9. Even though "they" is associated with the words of power such as "savage," the real and authentic power for action is associated with "us." The tyranny of "they" is buttressed in the third stanza in the image of "Orodje" and "Ogiso." In the footnote, these are tyrants from the historical past. Ogiso appears in the poem, "The Arrow Flight" in *Labyrinths of the Delta*, as "plagued dynasty of beast" (16-17) and in another poem, "Stone Culture" thus: "the Ogiso / wielding the stone culture of power" (30-31). Following the anthropological work of Tayo Olafioye, Niyi Akingbe has provided elaborate information on these two figures, Ogiso and Orodje. Akingbe goes on to read both *Labyrinths* and *The Endless Song* from the vantage position of New Historicism. He engages in exposing "the hidden hegemonic discourse embedded in Ojaide's poetry." He studies how Ojaide reconstructs historical materials in order to articulate the "ignoble wielding of power by Ogiso to oppress and traumatize his people." Furthermore, he avers that Ojaide employs snatches of Urhobo oral tradition and history to construct and expose the abuse of power in the Niger Delta" (Akingbe 9).

Readings such as that of Akingbe is pertinent. But as we had hinted earlier, it is a misreading of Ojaide's use of violence. Within the context of liminality, and in fact, the Niger Delta as a space of appropriation, Ojaide's focus is not on tyranny but the "they" that "savage us." His creative energy is dedicated to "us," the violence of those who have cast aside their "victimhood to become masters of their own lives." More crucially, the relics of Ogiso and Orodje are not just metaphors of tyranny, but against the current legacy of indirect rule within the Nigerian state vis-a-vis the crises surrounding the policy of indigeneity. They are fresh reminders to forces that are indirectly fanning the embers of "violence as the midwife of history." Again in the poem, "We Keep Watch over Them," only 6 lines refer to tyranny: lines 5, 9, 11, 12, 13 and 14. The aim in these lines is to recreate a picture of tyranny, like the annotated plaques from experience on the staircase of history, and to pitch against it, the iron will that drives the victims to their historical destiny of genuine freedom. We are told:

> There's metal in our will, it shows
> when we meet hardship—
> we do not break down before torturers
> we do not surrender our hope to robbers,
> we do not groan despite the daily stabs of hunger
> we do not give in to those who live on the blood
> of the poor or the sweat of strong (ll.19-25)

Observe that the "us" has now metamorphosed into "we," an appropriation and recreation of the victims' objective condition under tyranny to the position of "we," a subject and agent of action. Looking at these lines closely we cannot but agree that in Ojaide, Wole Soyinka's words, that "The man dies in all who keep silent in the face of tyranny," have found a recreation and appropriation in the space of Niger Delta.

Niger Delta as a Place of Hurt

Oil and gas explorations and expropriation in the Niger Delta region of Nigeria have brought many blessings, understood both in positive and negative terms. When we count the many and diverse blessings, the rise of militancy will break the records. Militancy has not only awakened us from the slumber to be more responsible in how we control the resources from oil and gas. Like the exploration activities that preceded it, it has spawned and initiated a second wave of displacement. The exploration of oil and gas has brought about massive pollution and the degradation of farmlands, rivers and waterways. These, in their wake, have displaced indigenous population from their farming and fishing activities. With their farmlands gone and the water ways and rivers either vanishing or dried up, these indigenous population drift to the urban centers like Port Harcourt and Yenagoa to find new and alternative means of livelihood.

The second wave of displacement is initiated by the rising culture of militancy in its many guises especially cultism. The clashes between many cult groups in semi-urban and rural communities have initiated a new wave of displacement whereby indigenes abandon their traditional village communities and migrate to find safety in cities as far away as Lagos, Port Harcourt or Abuja. While the multinational oil companies have devastated the natural environment, leading to the withering away of natural and local economy, the militant groups have exacerbated the trend by unleashing the withering away of the cultural values and indigenous symbolic capital that define the people, in what Onookome Okome has earlier referred to as the "desecration of divinity" (Okome cited in Shija 85). In this two-pronged attack on its land, and its cultural values, the Niger Delta has become a ticking time bomb. The question then is: how has Ojaide's poetry responded or represented this culture of hurt or condition of unhappy consciousness? How do these redefine the Niger Delta as the in-between-space of the nation, the space of transition?

One of the dilemmas emanating from the "growing tendency for indigeneity to become the litmus test for rights in postcolonial Nigeria" (Mamdani 657) is the increasing transformation of the space of the Niger Delta into a capitalist commodity economy that is based on petroleum. This economic turn, while transforming the Niger Delta as "the treasure base of the nation," has wrought displacement and hurt to the human and physical environment. The rush for material gains has entrapped indigenous population "trembling in the balance." It is the condition of hurt in the liminal space of the nation that provokes the imagination of Ojaide and ultimately, his poetry in the second phase. Thus in the poem, "The Music of Pain," published in *The Fate of Vultures and Other Poems*, the persona engages the reader in a passionate declaration as he candidly bemoans his experience in the threshold. The mood is meditative and grave. The poem is cast in the form of a dramatic monologue as the persona explains the basis of his pain. The technique of dramatic monologue does not only enable the persona to address the reader but also to interact with an implied reader in the text of the poem itself. This interaction is achieved through subtle clues in the poem. For example in lines 22 and 23 we are told: "'What can songs do?' they mocked me. / And I say.' Here we witness a mimetic enactment as the implied reader, other than the persona, rhetorically asks: "What can songs do?" and the persona responds: "And I say." As we listen to him, his tone reflects the knowledge of someone who has been there and who is a truthful witness of the pain and the indignity of dwelling in the liminal space.

In terms of structure, the poem is a free verse, organized in 34 lines and twelve sentences. The poem begins in an anaphoric opening and builds up to a crescendo, followed by the expression of doubt, which is neutralized by a fervent defence, and a conclusion. We will follow this structural pattern in our analysis. But it is important to note that as we follow the persona, we can picture him possibly sitting disconcertedly in a corner while unburdening his pain.

The first line begins with the word "Listen." This serves as an apostrophe and functions as a call to his listeners. Having arrested the listener's attention, he asserts: "I do not cry in vain. / For my song I sought/the chorus of resistant cries/ to excoriate the land's scurvy conscience" (ll. 2-5). The use of the first person pronoun in this opening section, in lines 2-3, underscores his subjectivity and sense of confidence even in his perturbed state. This sense of subjectivity is maintained in the second part, between lines 6 to 18, using the first person. However, in this segment, he unveils a series of actions taken thus: "I invoked Aridon," "I dressed my words with steel shafts." The use of the active verbs, "invoked" and "dressed" testifies to the self-assuredness of the speaking voice. Between lines 14 to 18, he recounts the outcome of his cry and song on the community. Thus we are told:

> My songs became the land's infantry
> drawing into its veins
> the strength of million;
> it took the cause of the country
> into its expanding heart.

Observe the juxtaposition of "songs" with "infantry." In other words, his songs became an army powerful enough to arrest the heart of millions who arose to defend the cause of the country. Observe also that the persona places country adjacent to land. I think that this implies that the multitude in the liminal space that have been touched by the power of his song have taken up its resonance. His songs become a veritable instrument of mobilization. This conveys the idea of the nature of the commitment of the poet in a postcolonial nation. Commitment here means what the poet is answerable to. As we can see through his poetry, Ojaide is ardently committed to the plight of the displaced who are literally trembling in the balance of social injustice. He illustrates the power of his mobilization; thus he asserts: "You can hear the rhythm ... / drummers telescope the vision/of a fate-lift to laughter" (ll.19-21). Ojaide has used not only words but even punctuation marks to great effect. Thus in line 19, the anacoluthon (- -) is used to imply a record of other effects produced by the tenor of his song.

A doubt is raised in the fourth segment as another voice interjects by asking: "What can songs do"? "They mock me". This sense of doubt provokes a defence from the persona. In his defence, he affirms not only what his song is but equally what it has done. Thus, he asserts the following:

"They have the bite of desperate ones" (ll. 24).

"They are fine-filed machetes" (ll. 25).

"They are a swarm of mystery bees haunting robbers of the proud heritage!" (ll. 27-28).

This is followed by a declaration of what his song has done: "My song has captured the roar of lions / and the jungle mortars of elephants" (ll. 29-30). In the concluding part, he returns to the use of apostrophe, followed with a pensive explanation: "Listen/A fortyish man does not cry in vain" (ll. 31-32). The success of the poem manifests not only in the skilful use of punctuation marks, techniques of oral discourse and dramatic monologue but also in the use of both visual and auditory images. For example, the persona asserts that his songs: "became the land's infantry" (ll.14), "fine-filed machetes" (ll.), "a swarm of mystery bees" (ll.), and "my song has captured the roar of lions/and the jungle mortars of elephants" (ll. 29-30). Besides, even though the persona speaks in the first person, which is an indication of his subjectivity, his voice projects communal pain and this is reiterated in the last two lines of the poem, thus: "listen to my song / the music of communal pain" (ll.34).

The pain and the frustration which we witness in "The Music of Pain" gather momentum in the poem, "No Longer Our Own Country," which appears in the collection, *The Blood of Peace and Other Poems*. Although published in the later collection in 1991, the poem was written in October 1986. We will attempt a close reading of the poem and engage in an interpretation that is in line with the preoccupation with the theme of hurt recorded in the poetry of the second phase.

"No Longer Our Own Country" is a poem of 53 lines and arranged in five stanzas. It is rendered in the first person plural form, "we" and its possessive form, "our: "We have lost it / the country we were born into" (ll.1-2). Reading through this poem in 2018, against the backdrop of current historical and political realities in Nigeria and especially in the Niger Delta, is like living through the fulfilment of an ominous prophecy. Although written way back in 1986, Ojaide fulfils his role not only as a legislator but his duty as a prophet (*vate* and seer). In this poem, he foresaw the current atmosphere of violence that has ravaged the nation and the Niger Delta region. All the symptoms of this culture of violence, including the internal displacement of indigenes from their ancestral homelands, not only due to oil exploration and pollution, but also due to politically and cult motivated wars. Following from these internecine wars that would make Yambo Oueloguem's *Bound to Violence* seem like a mere child's play is the destruction of the people's symbolic capital, the erosion of the values and customs that give the people their sense of identity as a people. In the poem, the persona captures this erosion in the image of "our totem eagle, that bird of great heights/has been shot by the thoughtless guardians" (ll. 9-10). Sociologists, including Emile Durkheim, have demonstrated that it is these aspects of a people's symbolic capital that guarantee a sense of organic solidarity. The persona laments also of "our flag ripped off by uncaring hands" (ll.13) and he bemoans: "Where are those warriors / careful not to break taboos" (ll. 23-24).

The poem directly deals with the problem of internal displacement. Available records, as of 2017, show that approximately 1,770,444 people were displaced in the North East as a result of the ongoing conflict against insurgency in that region (Mohammed 6). Apart from the North East, the Niger Delta has witnessed internal displacement in recent years especially between 2014 and 2017. There are two main drivers of displacement in the Niger Delta, according to the report by Fatima Kyari Mohammed. These are social drivers and environmental drivers. Under the social drivers, there are inter-communal clashes, criminality leading to "rural banditry," while the major factor under the environmental drivers is oil spillage. It is estimated that, as of 2016, a total number of over 300,000 people were displaced in the Niger Delta (Mohammed 6). The records above testify that there is sufficient ground for the concern expressed in the poem, "No Longer Our Own Country." Thus we are told: "now we are exiles / in a country that was once ours-" (35-36). Underlying this declaration is that deep psychological sense of loss, of being caught in-between being and *not* being. It is a loss that has crushed our hope for a commonwealth and a sense of community. Ojaide envisions healing and recovery even in the deep loss. He is convinced that the loss will engender knowledge and a new orientation to appreciate what we have and to preserve it. Thus we are told: "we now know / what it is to lose our home / what it is to lose a hospitable place" (ll. 45-47).

Conclusion

This is a study of how Ojaide has negotiated the link between literary production, life and the environment, especially in the second phase of his poetry which is focused on the crises and disillusionment associated with leadership in Nigeria. This study argues that the appropriation of a legacy of British colonial policy of indirect rule has recreated the nature of rights and access to privileges in postcolonial Nigeria. The consequence is that a section of the population is abandoned in the in-between space of the nation. By adopting the postcolonial theory of liminality, this study has analyzed and reinterpreted selected poems of Ojaide as representation of the Niger Delta as a space of hurt.

Works Cited

Anderson, Benedict. *Imagined Communities*: *Reflections on the Origin and Spread of Nationalism.* Verso, 2006.

Ake, Claude. *A Political Economy of Africa.* Longman Group, 1981.

Akingbe, Niyi. "A battle cry against depravity: Lamenting generational dispossession in Tanure Ojaide's *Labyrinths of the Delta* and *Endless Song*". *Imbizo: International Journal of African Literary and Comparative Studies.* Vol. 5 No 1 (2014): 3-22.

Ashcroft, Bill, Gareth Griffiths and Helen Tiffin.*Post-Colonial Studies: The Key Concepts*. Routledge, 2000.

——————. *The Empire Writes Back: Theory and Practice in Postcolonial Literature.* Routledge, 1989.

Bhabha, Homi. *The Location of Culture.* London: Routledge, 1994.

——————. "Introduction: Narrating the Nation". In *Nation and Narration*.Ed. Homi Bhabha. Routledge, 1990:1-7.

Coundouriotis, Eleni. "The Historical Novel in Africa".In *The Novel in Africa and the Caribbean since 1950,* Ed. Simon Gikandi. Oxford: Oxford University Press, 2016:269-284.

Eliot, T.S. "Tradition and the Individual Talent". In *The Norton Anthology of Theory &Criticism.*General Editor, Vincent B. Leitch. W.W. Norton & Company, 2001:1092-1098.

Fanon, Frantz. *The Wretched of the Earth.* Penguin, 1952.

Gelven, Michael. *A Commentary on Heidegger's Being and Time.* Northern Illinois University Press, 1989.

Hogue, Rebecca. "Cultural Identity and Liminal Places in Contemporary Literature of Hawai'i".*Rocky Mountain Review*, Special Issue (2012):144-152.

Loomba, Ania. *Colonialism/Postcolonialism.* Routledge, 1998.

Mamdani, Mahmoud. "Beyond Settler and Native as Political Identities: Overcoming the Political Legacy of Colonialism". *Society for Comparative Study of Society and History* 2001: 651-664.

————————."Making Sense of Political Violence in Postcolonial Africa".*Identity, Culture and Politics*. Vol. 3 No. 2 (2002): 1-24.

Mbembe, Achille. *On the Postcolony*. University of California Press, 2001.

Mohammed, Fatima Kyari. "The Causes and Consequences of Internal Displacement in Nigeria and Related Governance Challenges". *Working Papers*, FG 18, SWP-Berlin, April, 2017.

Nwoga, D.I. "Modern African Poetry: The Domestication of a Tradition". African Literature Today, No 10 (1979):32-56.

Ojaide, Tanure. *The Endless Song*. Malthouse Press Limited, 1989.

————————. *The Fate of Vultures and Other Poems*. Malthouse Press Limited, 1990.

————————. *The Blood of Peace and Other Poems*. Heinemann Educational Books (Nigeria) Ltd, 1991.

Rozelle, Lee. "Resurveying Delillo's "White Space on Map": Liminality and Communitas in *Underworld*".*Studies in the Novel* Vol. 42 No. 4 (2010):443-452.

Sallah, Tijan. "The Eagle's Vision: The Poetry of Tanure Ojaide". *Research in African Literatures* Vol. No.

Shija, Terhemba. *Post-Coloniality and the Poetry of Tanure Ojaide*. Aboki Publishers, 2006.

Nostalgia as Aesthetic in Tanure Ojaide's *In the House of Words*

Saeedat B. Aliyu

Introduction

The investigation of nostalgia as an aesthetic in Ojaide's *In the House of Words* takes off from the postulations of psychologists such as Sigmund Freud and Sedikides et al. These psychologists opine that nostalgia is a psychological state engendered by initially negative emotional state but which gives rise to positive feelings especially through the recreation of the reality of the individual's choice. As a psychological investigation into the thoughts of a poet-persona, this present study is concerned with the triggers of nostalgia and with his attempts at recreating a physical and socio-economic space he desires. It is concerned also with the ways the persona encounters and interprets his memories.

This study engages with Buttler's categorization of nostalgic perspectives into experiential and politicized (9). To her, experiential nostalgia entails honoring attachments and losses. It is a melancholic enactment of notable past experiences and it entails recollections that are not influenced by societal values or biases. Politicized nostalgia on the other hand involves recollections influenced by cultural values and symbols. It is nostalgia which reveals an individual's cultural biases and these biases implicate constructions of positive or negative affect. The present study explores both perspectives in the melancholic recollections of the poet- persona as there are instances in the collection where the poet's melancholia of memories is without cultural signification. In these instances, the persona explores feelings that are not subjected to cultural or societal validation. Rather, they are reminiscences of past events that are notable to the persona. In other instances, the persona reads and sustains cultural beliefs in his memories and upholds these values as the ultimate state.

The subsequent sections of this paper explore nostalgia as aesthetic; an exploration into theoretical/psychological implications of nostalgia and how Ojaide deploys it to push his ideology about the society.

Nostalgia as Aesthetic

Sigmund Freud in "Creative Writers and Day-Dreamers" opines that part of the burden of growing up is the forfeiture of the pleasures of play. The pleasures of play for adults are then realized through day-dreams and phantasies which he says are avenues to emerge from the unsatisfactory realities of daily existence. Sedikides et al. also theorize that negative mood and loneliness are everyday emotional experiences which generate positive affects through the mental creation of alternative realities. Both postulations identify that the search for pleasure or positive feelings generate the creation of alternative realities. It is this psychological search for pleasure, for positive feelings, that encapsulates the term "nostalgia." Nostalgia is thus taken to be a feeling of loss, a longing, a yearning for something, an incompleteness or a dissatisfaction with current state which evolves into the recreation or reimagining of an ideal alternative that ameliorates the initial negative feeling.

What this study is concerned with in Freud's postulation is that nostalgia prompts fantasies, the creation of worlds where individuals find fulfillment of dreams. Freud goes on to identify three moments which facilitate day dreaming. They are: provocations in a person's present or reality; the arousal of memories and thoughts to negate the reality; and, the creation of a future ideal situation where the fulfillment of wishes is achieved. Sedikides et al. also assert that nostalgia serves four psychological functions: of generating positive affect; of elevating self-esteem; of bringing about social connectedness; and of alleviating existential threats by helping the individual to "navigate successfully the vicissitudes of daily life" (307).

The nostalgic musings of the poet-persona in the selected collection is triggered by his introspections during solitary encounters with everyday experiences. These musings contain feelings of negative affects which arise from realities that are unsatisfactory to him. These mental journeys, wishes, and revelations avail the poet-persona the avenue to contrast current unsatisfactory realities with stored images of a more positive time. By making reference to previous encounters, the persona juxtaposes these stored images with contemporary realities. This affords him the platform to recreate the experiences he desires. In this case, the musings do not only serve the poet persona's individualistic aspirations but include his vision on social issues that go beyond the individual. As an aesthetic, it furthers the functional role of African literary art as it enables the recreation of social orders that advance society.

Drawing from the postulations of Freud and Sedikides et al, we begin our investigation of nostalgia in the selected collection of poems by highlighting the provocations in the poet-persona's immediate reality. This is followed by the identification and examination of the memories or thoughts to negate the unsatisfactory reality; and then an examination of how the persona creates a future where he fulfills his desires.

Provocations of Nostalgia in *In the House of Words*

Sedikides et al. identify loneliness as one of the two provocations of nostalgia. Ojaide evokes this state early in his collection. It is the loneliness of the persona that sets the stage for nostalgic reminiscences in the first poem of the collection entitled "Simple Songs" (1). The poem reads like the prologue to a story, like a narrator setting the tone of a coming event. This is significant as it marks the commencement of the persona's psychological wanderings throughout most of the collection. The poet makes the persona subconsciously embark on a mental journey back in time and space. This is where the coalescion of experiential and politicized remembrance begins. The collection under study details an actual journey of the poet from Charlotte in the United States back to his homeland and other places he visited on that particular trip to Nigeria. This presents avenues for the poet to evoke both culture-free and culture-induced experiences.

Two strategically placed poems trail the lonely state established in the prologue poem. These poems, "Night in Charlotte" (3-4) and "I Grew Tired of Towers" (5-6), are the first two poems in the collection and they foreground the disconnection between the persona and the non-African abode in the United States. Dissatisfaction with the persona's environmental reality in the poems prompts a craving for a re-experience of the ancestral environment. In "I Grew Tired of Towers" (5-6), Ojaide underscores features of the Charlotte environment that cause dissatisfaction to the persona. In this poem, his discontent is caused by the dominance of an impersonal and commoditized environment typified by towers, steel, concrete, spires, white-and-blue-eyed lights - all artificial, sterile, impersonal objects - which overshadow the natural environment. Here we see an underlying craving for the personalized and natural feel of African communities. The capitalist society adds a strain to the realization of the persona's desires as it encourages the degradation of plant and animal life in "Night in Charlotte" where he describes souls as depressed and the glitter of stars stifled by satellites (3). This impersonal and nature-disinclined environment contrasts with the communal and spiritual environment in which the poet had his childhood.

The contrasting imagery of his communal, natural, and spiritual ancestral home is established in poems such as "Night in Charlotte" (3-4), "In the Shadow of the Iroko" (11-13) and "The Homeboy Suite" (16-24). This is why he states his longing for a "return / to the home he was born into fifty years ago / to be born again into fresh water whose flow / keeps the heart pounding with youthful zest" ("I Grew Tired of Tower" 6). These poems underscore the persona's discontent and they describe what Freud calls an "unsatisfying reality" and Sedikides et al. refer to as "negative mood."

"Night in Charlotte," for instance is a comparison between the nightline in Charlotte and the poet's ancestral home. In the comparison, night in Charlotte falls short on every count. The poet describes night in Charlotte as: "without the tongue of darkness," "defaced by neon lights," "marooned in the company of depressed souls," "wet from the tears of a dethroned moon," "incapable of playing hide-and-seek," "that does not gather children at home," "without dreams," and "without ghosts" (3). These descriptions underscore how night in Charlotte represents an unsatisfying reality and they reflect both experiential and politicized perspectives. Ojaide infuses into the descriptions the persona's individualized conceptions of night-time experienced while in his ancestral homeland. The tone of loss is distinct in the images evoked. It echoes the persona's loss of experiences which were touchstones in his youth. It also reveals the politicization of the concept of night. The descriptions show a cultural inflection that personifies and spiritualizes night, imbuing it with the mysticism of indigenous cultures. These include images of a vibrant night-time which he experienced in his childhood in Nigeria; they come to the fore in the poem:

> There are no masquerades patrolling the night
> no witches flying spacecraft of groundnut shells
> no spirits assembled at crossroads to feast on sacrifices
> and with guttural tirades chill the hearts of women and children.
> … no *otie* tree lays a lavish feast at its feast
> no palm tree gushes wine to carouse with ("Night in Charlotte" 3)

The prominent use of the negative marker 'no' in those lines highlight the many features that are absent in the night life of Charlotte. It also encapsulates the extent of the poet-persona's desire to reacquaint himself with his ancestral home.

Worthy of note also is the preponderant evocation of inadequacy and loneliness. The poet employs those images to propel the persona into the search for touchstones, either physically or through memories, which will assuage his desires for a re-experiencing of his ancestral home. Images from memory in this case become the strategy the persona deploys and thus forms the bedrock for his introspection about his existence in places away from the ancestral home.

Memory as Counter-Strategy

The engagement with memories of a pristine environment drawn from the persona's childhood help negate the unsatisfactory realities which confront him and serve as a strategy to overcome the agitations in his contemporary realities.

This is in spite of the fact that the capitalist mindset has spread and taken root even in his native home as he states in "I Grew Tired of Towers":

> The migrant returns. He takes an old road
> round and round his house without seeing it.
> Groves have given way to highways,
> Wetlands, aviaries and ponds reclaimed
> for opulent mansions and housing estates
> that place politicians and contractors on one side.

This reliance on images stored in the subconscious is the strategy to counter the desolation of his existence. This is why, in "I Took a Boat" (7-8), Ojaide depicts a reconnection with features such as the village of the persona's birth, the water he swam in as a child, the cherry tree underneath which he and his friends played, the ditties of frogs, birds and rain, the moon, and the Omwe stream among others.

In "The Homeboy Suite" (16-24) also, the poet recounts his boyhood activities and the wisdom of oral traditions he learnt as a youth. In "A Trip to a Traditional Library" (28-30), the persona expresses the desire to glean wisdom from Ogbariemu, the octogenarian. He dubs such wisdom as "texts of remembrance" (30), bodies of knowledge stored in human memory. This is synonymous to the memories the poet stores in his subconscious which he recalls during nostalgic moments. In this poem, the persona concedes that while Ogbariemu personifies a well-stocked library (filled with knowledge, wisdom and details from the days of his great grandfather), he also embodies knowledge of stereotypes inimical especially to the female gender and the Christian faith. It is a similar stereotyping that a natural haven exists in the poet's ancestral environment that he relies upon in periods of desolation. These are politicized memories which add to the values of the images.

Other poems in the collection record the persona's re-encounter with familiar features of the environment. Poems such as "Savannah Suite" (51-57), "Mararaba, Abuja Nearby" (58-59), "Welcome Song" and "Sunday Morning in the University Park" (85-56).

Recreating Alternative Futures

As Freud espouses that when there is an unsatisfactory present and a reactionary arousal of memories of a more acceptable experience, what follows is the creation of a future or a phantasy where the fulfillment of such wishes is achieved: "Thus past, present and future are strung together, as it were, on the thread of the wish that runs through them" (Freud 424). Freud advances this theory by stating that:

We must not suppose that the products of this imaginative activity —the various phantasies, castles in the air and day-dreams—are stereotyped or unalterable. On the contrary, they fit themselves in to the subject's shifting impressions of life, change with every change in his situation, and receive from every fresh active impression what might be called a "date-mark" (421-2).

Indeed, Ojaide depicts this shifting impression as there are indications of multiple wishful creations. These creations draw significantly from the cultural values interspersed with individualized conceptualizations.

For instance, in "An Old Yearning Grips Me" (9-10), the poet promotes an awareness of the capitalist inflections of the many wishes expressed in the poem. Prominent among the wishes include the desire to return the economic focus of his native region back to what it was by:

Dredg[ing] the Ethiope River deep and wide
to put back ships and pontoons that kept Sapele alive…
I want John Holt and UAC in their river-port stations
to boldly mark Okpari town on the new maps (9)

Other yearnings capture the effects of capitalism. He desires therefore to rid his locality of the despoliation caused by crude oil exploration: "I want to be an Area Boy in Okurekpo of long ago / to chase out Shell-BP from dispossessing villagers" (9). In other fantasies, Ojaide reveals his desires to relive the euphoria of a new independent nation, the deep wish for patriots like Essi to motivate other patriots who can stop the corrupt tendencies in the country, and to fulfill the desires of Nigerians at the turn of the independence. One desire that also stands out is his desire to relive his childhood, to re-experience the innocence and communal nature of his childhood. Lines like "I want the double-decker bus back on the –Sapele Road / to play in it before it fills up at its stop across the river" (9), support Freud's thesis that:

As people grow up, then, they cease to play, and they **seem to give up** the yield of pleasure which they gained from playing. But whoever understands the human mind knows that hardly anything is harder for a man than to give up a pleasure which he has once experienced. Actually, we can never give anything up; we only exchange one thing for another. What appears to be a renunciation is really the formation of a substitute or surrogate. In the same way, the growing child, when he stops playing, gives up nothing but the link with real objects; instead of *playing,* he now *phantasies*. (**emphasis mine,** 422)

The poet persona's craving for his childhood therefore extends beyond his personal need. His desire to influence some perceived wrongs in his childhood is seminal. For instance, he states that Owhesiri was denied the crown as the belle of the new Miss Universe pageant and also he wishes to save Titi's father from committing suicide because of some debts. This reliving of childhood is also a strategy to correct wrongs done at a period the persona had no means of influencing such situations. Ojaide furthers the expression of this desire in "The Homeboy Suite" when he states that: "I am still hungry for the same home dish / that I missed in search of what I couldn't find" (16). In this poem and "The Community Development Officer," the poet goes beyond his personal needs to address societal issues like endemic cheating, corruption, religious fanatism, and obsessions with technology.

Conclusion

Through an investigation of the aesthetics of nostalgia in Ojaide's *In the House of Words,* Sedikides et al's position that nostalgia serves psychological functions: of generating positive affect; of elevating self-esteem; of bringing about social connectedness; and, of alleviating existential threats by helping the individual to "navigate successfully the vicissitudes of daily life" (307) is realized. By employing images of an ideal time, the poet is able to overcome the negative feelings overwhelming him. As a committed literary artist, Ojaide uses this aesthetic to further his vision for a better society; he relives and creates alternative images of social realities.

Works Cited

Buttler, T.M. "Learning the Languages of Nostalgia in Modern and Contemporary Literature." A PhD Dissertation, University of Washington, USA, 2012.

Ojaide, Tanure. *In the House of Words.* Lagos: Malthouse, 2013.

Sedikides, C. Tim Wildschut, Jamie Arndt, and Clay Routledge. "Nostalgia: Past, Present, and Future". *Current Directions in Psychological Science,* Association for Psychological Science. Volume 17—Number 5, 2008, 304-307.

Sigmund, Freud. "Creative Writers and Day-Dreaming." Translated by Joan Riviere. The Hogarth Press Ltd.

Environmental Activism and Poetry:

Tanure Ojaide's *The Tale of the Harmattan*

Honoré Missihoun

Introduction

Ojaide uses *The Tale* as a subaltern communication to give a voice to marginalized people in society by re-focalizing and subverting hegemonic discourse through narrations that authentically articulate the people's identities, interests, anxieties and dedications.

The *harmattan* becomes a sustained metaphor for the devastation that has come to characterize Africa, Nigeria, the Niger Delta in particular, and the corruption reflected in the people, especially the government. In telling the tale, Ojaide makes puns upon words and asks whether this is the tail of the *harmattan*: Are we at the end? Is there a hope? Or is there no light at the end of the tunnel? In analyzing these questions and poems relating to them, this paper explores how Ojaide employs irony, metaphor, *réécriture* or poetics of repetition to embrace the dichotomy that his tale encapsulates, and his belief that the human mind is amenable to instruction and can be led towards love of the natural environment.

The paper acknowledges, as critic Uzoechi Nwagbara puts it in his work, Ojaide's aesthetic insights and unfathomable poetic prowess to reconstruct social facts thereby bringing to mankind everywhere through poetic songs the scrapes, exploitation, dehumanization, and for the foremost part, the dehistoricization of the people of Niger Delta and of Nigeria at large. *The Tale* is in the main a clarion call to intensify the struggles aimed at averting ecological genocide, what the martyred eco-activist and author, Ken Saro-Wiwa referred to as "ecological war" in *Genocide in Nigeria*. Ojaide's program of actions to this end is in phases: private, local, and global. Even though it is largely poetry of "anguish and complaint," Ojaide has, however, crafted in these lines the framework to achieve freedom in the midst of socio-economic turmoil and politico-cultural labyrinth. It is surely one of his greatest works of negating social contradictions which can help us to look in new ways at the literary project of imagining effective struggles for environmental justice in the Delta region, in Nigeria, and in Africa. This aesthetic commitment is echoed in one of the poems, "The Egbesu Boys," which identifies with the plights of the masses of the people to bring change via the instrumentality of negation of social realities in their devastated natural environment made possible by the federal government and faceless multinationals, even the ruling elite. In a nutshell, the totality of *The Tale* paints a bleak picture of the people of the Delta and of Nigeria in general, albeit some hope seems to appear on the horizon.

In his work, Dike Okoro writes: "Absorbing, startling and uncannily pitched to public and private issues that penetrate the social climate and upheaval of present-day Nigeria and Africa might be the best way to describe prolific Nigerian scholar-poet, Tanure Ojaide's new poetry collection, *The Tale of Harmattan.*" Published in South Africa by the prestigious Kwela Books of Cape Town, the book contains three sections and has a glossary that spares the reader unfamiliar with the terrain of Nigeria's landscape, politics, and Urhobo folklore the pain of leafing through such a fine collection without knowledge of the references made to mythical and historical figures.

The Niger Delta's Plight in the Poet's Intimate Sensibility

Part One of T*he Tale*, much like Ojaide's previous poetry collections, narrates and reflects on local issues with global implications. We learn the precarious story of oil drilling which continues to dog Nigeria's collective conscience.Ojaide aestheticizes a series of struggles for a healthy environment, multinational corporations'sensibility to indigenes in their business transactions, minority rights, rights of natives to be treated as humans, and the legacy of grandmothers. But what makes this section of *The Tale* fulfilling is not the attention given to issues overlapping politics but the poet's highly aestheticized and memorable free verses. In a more postcolonial context, and in his effort to address growing despair and frustration, like other Niger Delta poets, namely Nnimmo Bassey and Ogaga Ifowodo,Ojaide has drawn on and transformed Saro-Wiwa's narratives of resistance. Like Saro-Wiwa, Ojaide foregrounds the injustice of neoliberal globalization and stresses the possibility of finding inspiration among the people of the Delta. At the same time, he points to the limitations of ethnic identity, offers an open-ended conceptualization of resistance, and refuses the role of an authoritative sage in ways Saro-Wiwa did not (Caminero-Santangelo 170)). In the process, he revitalizes Saro-Wiwa's project of imagining an alternative trajectory of development in the Niger Delta.A closer look at *The Tale* shows that while older Nigerian poets have explored the relationship between human beings and the natural environment, the poetry of Ojaide makes a more direct connection between art and activism by confronting the destructive extraction of crude oil in the Niger Delta.To fulfill his poetic mission of imagining an alternative strategy to Saro-Wiwa's socio ecological development, Ojaide has recourse to the process of *réécriture*.

Following *Delta Blues and Home Songs*, some ten years later, *The Tale* finds Ojaide still "blue," as his former hopes have not been realized (Caminero-Santangelo 172). Published well after General Sani Abacha's death and return to democratic rule, and after almost a decade of growing armed conflict and continued socio-ecological anarchism, *The Tale* also finds the poet grappling with despair. It too is part of a Nigerian poetics of "lamentation" expressing "aestheticized rage in the form of sad songs" (Egya 102). However, the reasons for the poet's despair have shifted or are differently inflected as a result of the increasing violence in the Delta and the lack of improvement after Nigeria's shift to democratic rule in 1999; in turn, the grounding for hope he offers entails both inspiration and a clear departure from Saro-Wiwa.

The first poem of the collection, "The Goat Song," according to Ojaide's explanation in the glossary section of the book, "represents a song of anguish and complaint." Indeed, that statement is true when we examine the way he weaves sarcasm into couplets that reflect and philosophize the reality of living in the Niger Delta. The opening couplet reads: "I sing the community's goat song / Folks wear gold over tumours of hope." These lines are premeditated because they set the tone for the last two couplets of the first section of this poem as the reader becomes aware of what drives Ojaide's anguish and complaint when his speaker bemoans: "And who cares if foreigners found deep / under their bare feet divine gifts of pools / and started to tap the earth's underbelly / for fuel to blaze brushes of progress? (9)

Ojaide is also masterfully subtle in deploying imagery of monstrous transference to represent the geography of asymmetrical and uneven development, the exploitation of the Third World nations by the Northern countries. A vampire-like process of oil drilling and global distribution is imagined as sucking the life from the Niger Delta. Again, the repetition: "The blackened stream, ancestral blood / tapped away by giant pipes into ships / to rejuvenate foreign cities, invigorate markets" (10).

The Niger Delta Plight and Poems of Collective Conscious

Section two of the collection presents the poet as a public voice. The themes approached are both dynamic and very much related to events in today's Nigeria. Yet the poems come through as with any good poet's artistry. With the poems in this part, one can easily identify with the narrator's thirst and hunger for human freedom, his passion for his subject matter, his reflection on the injustices orchestrated against the Niger Delta people, their land, and their natural resources. In conspectus, the tragedy suffered in the destruction of wildlife and natural habitat is clearly examined with the skillful touch of a seasoned poet in this section of *The Tale,* which clearly gives each of the poems the universal appeal and attention reminiscent of any other ethnic group or culture whose natural habitat is threatened by petroleum pollution and incompetence in the circles of power. Here again, the poem, "At the Kaiama Bridge" jumps at the reader with a tone and subtlety contained in the direct appeal for the protection of natural resources when the narrator cries in stanza four:

> We have organized a resistance army,
> declared sovereignty over our resources;
> but have not pushed back the poachers.
> Outside forces pillage the inheritance. (33)

In the poem "For the Egbesu Boys" Ojaide's solidarity with the fight for the oppressed and dispossessed is clearly delineated in the verses: "For the same reason I sang praises of the Ogoni youths, I praise you Egbesu Boys in song – you cannot be / shackled from enjoying your own land's blessing; / you do the honorable duty of brave sons – fight on" (41). Here we can understand the ambivalence in Ojaide's lines while also noting his ingenious use of diction that is both exalting and gravitating. The poet protests against the bleak plight of the Niger Delta whose natural resources the Egbesu Boys are fighting for. More in support of the boys, Ojaide invokes the Ijo "War-god of born fishers and farmers [Egbesu] / to stand steadfast behind" (41) the Egbesu Boys who fight for what Ojaide calls elsewhere an "ecology of justice" that will counter the collusion between the Nigerian government and "multinational corporations to extract ... oil and gas without regard for the environment or wellbeing of local communities" (*Contemporary* 66, 77).

"The coalition of global powers" has destroyed the rivers, mangled harvests through gas flaring, poisoned the water and air with "insidious chemicals," and bred "an asthmatic and cancer-pronegeneration," "but boys" will not "sit and be enslaved" or "die without fighting back (41-42). Resistance, armed with the spirit of environmental "justice ... will always triumph in the prolonged battle," despite all the forces arrayed against it: "Those who bring a running fight to the iguana / will lose their breath and withdraw before long" (42). The proverb offers a promise of success in the long run through fortitude and patience and sums up the wisdom needed to overcome despair in the face of seemingly hopeless circumstances.

"The goat songs" of the collection – that is, the songs of anguish and complaint – focus on imperial exploitation fueled by a deceptive discourse of progress and salvation. Continuing the work of "Pentecostal converts" who burnt down the primeval grove" in a different colonial age, developers "tore down the forest" and trashed the natural canopies" in the name of the "foreign-accented god" of modernization: "they argued we needed roads to go out, as if we knew / nothing of adventure or did not visit other places" (12). Although "the government assures people of development," the vast majority is left with neither the riches of the past nor the benefits of modernity. There are no "scholarships" or "jobs for the graduates in the oil sector"; meanwhile, "wells litter the family's farmland," and the narrator's children cannot "fish or tap rubber as [he] once did" (22). Foreign capital and national elite reap their profits at the expense of the livelihoods, the health, and the futures of the Delta's people: "We know the capital gain from the blessed but besieged land will go down the drain for a caste to maintain its smug smile" (13). Reversing the development narrative, the narrator claims they have entered a "new Stone Age" of primitive capitalist accumulation "with refilled slave ships refurbished as super-tankers / anchored at Escravos and poaching inland as centuries ago" (22).

In the poem "Transplants," the eponymous metaphor figures the process by which the United States benefits from petro-driven modernity and still preserves its ecological riches by creating an environmental apocalypse elsewhere. In the Delta, "the forest fell / foul to fires of oil blowouts and poaching raids," and "the creek [he] fished in without care" are "now clogged" (39). Meanwhile, in the United States, the kind of natural beauty and biological diversity he associates with the forest landscape of his youth are preserved: "the pristine streams, the multiethnic population / of plants, costumed birds, and graceful game" (39). Seeing both landscapes together through the eye of imagination helps to highlight their connection: "In a half-century one world disappeared; another persists. / Only outside do I now see the landscape of my childhood" (39). In the context of economic globalization, environmental preservation in the affluent lands of the North cannot be separated from ecological catastrophe in the Global South. Through such double vision, Ojaide subtly undoes pastoral tropes of retreat by emphasizing the impossibility of separating nature from monstrously unjust transnational relationships.

Other poems in section two also reminiscent of the anguish and complaint which sustain the intensity of the entire *The Tale* are "Dialogue," "Without Trees," and "Swimming in a Waterhole". It will be fair at this juncture to say that the poems position *The Tale* as a work that reflects the poet's Niger Delta environmental experiences. From an ecostylistic perspective, Ojaide employs free verse and vernacular lexical features as well as various figures of expression to project his environmental message and make his work lucid. Stylistic analysis relates features of linguistic description to aspects of critical interpretation of a text. In this sense, *The Tale*, a subaltern communication, resists the imposition of "Western" theory onto African artistic practices that *The Tale* epitomizes. It uses theory against itself, and from a poststructuralist perspective, it rejects approaches of fidelity and medium specificity in favor of a notion of *réécriture* or poetics of repetition. Indeed, many of the poems comfortably and eloquently straddle part one and part two of *The Tale,* expressing various and context-specific sensibilities of the poet. Such is the case of "The Priests, Converts, and Gods", "The Egbesu Boys", and "Transplants".

Faced with growing socioecological violence and despair, Ojaide and other new Niger Delta poets such as Ogaga Ifowodo overtly align themselves with Ken Saro-Wiwa and, at the same time, deviate from a number of his conclusions. Indeed, the dichotomy in the choice of these new poets invites reflection on the notion of *réécriture* or poetics of repetition.

Approaching *The Tale* from poststructuralist angle, I will say along with Tcheuyap that Ojaide aims to dismantle the deterministic authorial and media-imposed power relations constructed by conventional writing adaptation theory. Tcheuyap argues that, "The concern is… not the subjugation of a medium or a text, but that of the various *"creative, poetic and ideological process implied in the repetition that brings change to any rewriting,"* (3).Tcheuyap's definition of repetition is one that incorporates difference and that clearly does not locate itself within discourses around modernity's modes of automatic, repetitive production. Like Tcheuyap, Ojaide tries to calibrate his writing adaptation to the context of repetition with difference, repetition as a result of human agency rather than the simulacra of technological and industrial machinery. In short, *The Tale* engages Ojaide in discourse production processes known as "change in continuity" dear to Chinua Achebe, and "signifin(g)" by Henry Gates.

The Poet and Poetic of Human Concerns

The last section of *The Tale* is sentimental, euphonious, and forewarning. Ojaide's narrator navigates issues fueled by private and public concerns. The themes covered here are thought-provoking, emotional, and foreshadowing. The brilliance of this section can be seen in Ojaide's mastery at blending oral tradition with western poetic forms.

The verses are free, yet there is a seriousness of purpose that rekindles their intensity, making each poem memorable for the reader. In the fiery and angry "To the Janjaweed," we notice and feel the poet's empathy with the victims and his resentment for the predators. Crafted in a tradition of abuse poetry, Ojaide chides and derides the notorious killing gang responsible for much of the deaths in Sudan's Darfur region. Each couplet in this poem is rich with memorable images and utterances as the poet laments:

> May the fire you spread gleefully this way
> scorch you and your family at the other end
>
> may your patrons in government corridors
> become dead vultures to the entire world
>
> may the horses you ride to sack villages
> throw you into vainglorious days … (58)

The same emotional intensity Ojaide shows in the above-mentioned poem is sustained in the other poems in this section. The only difference is in the shift from public to the private voice. For example, the poem "Remembering," a tribute to a dead friend, clearly exhibits the dexterity and virtuoso of a poet. The images are very striking, and the last line gives the poem a memorable closing strength as Ojaide avers:

> The day all alarms refused to do off
> the day the clear-eyed guide lost his vision
>
> the day the boneless beast opened its mouth
> to swallow an entire man like sautéed crayfish
>
> that day was the day of the summer solstice when in
> Jerusalem my best friend died in Sapele. (57)

Conclusion

By the end of *The Tale,* it is clear to the reader what Ojaide has set out to accomplish with his aesthetic production. His move from personal and local concerns to national, universal, and human issues evinces how grounded he is with historical memory.

The ecological devastation in the Niger Delta remains mostly invisible to an international community focused more on oil security than on human rights or environmental injustice. In his efforts to address the growing despair and frustration, Ojaide has drawn on and transformed Ken Saro-Wiwa's narratives of resistance. Like him, he foregrounds the injustice of neoliberal globalization and stresses the possibility of finding inspiration among the peoples of the Niger Delta; at the same time, he points to the limitations of ethnic identity, offers an open-ended conceptualization of resistance, and refuses the role of an authoritative sage in the ways Saro-Wiwa did not. In the process, Ojaide revitalizes Saro-Wiwa's project of imagining an alternative trajectory of development in the Niger Delta through the critical writing strategy of *réécriture* or poetics of repetition.

It is now safe to affirm that Ojaide walks in the footstep of Saro-Wiwa and follows the critical principle of "change in continuity." In this sense, he is engaged in a process of what Henry Louis Gates calls "signifyin(g)." According to Gates, signifyin(g) "functions as a metaphor for formal revision, or intertextuality" (xxi); it is repetition with a difference. If Ojaide's revision foregrounds homage and continuity (rather than disjuncture), he still, like Achebe's model of cultural production, entails significant, even extravagant aberration (Caminero-Santangelo 182).

We enjoy *The Tale* for all its aesthetic and artistic worth. The language, though highly sophisticated, is simple and reminiscent of the poet's talent. With the publication of *The Tale*, Ojaide has become part of Kwela Books' coterie of major authors singing Africa's song from local to the global.

Works Cited

Achebe, Chinua. *Arrow of God*. Anchor, 1964.

Caminero-Santangelo, Byron. *Different Shades of Green: African Literature, Environmental Justice, and Political Ecology*. University of Virginia Press, 2014.

Egya, Sule Emmanuel. "The Aesthetic of Rage of Rage in Recent Nigerian Poetry in English: Olu Oguibe and Ifowodo Ogaga."
Matatu: Journal of African Culture and Society 39.2 (2011): 99-114.

Gates, Henry Louis. *The Signifying Monkey*. Oxford UP, 1988.

Ifowodo, Ogaga. *The Oil Lamp*. Africa World Press, 2005.

Nwagbara, Uzoechi www.aftricanwriter.comojaide-sings-the-tale-of-the-hartmann-from-cape-town/

Ojaide, Tanure.*The Tale of the Harmattan*. Kwela Books / Snailpress, 2007.

———*Contemporary African Literature: New Approaches*. Carolina Academic Press, 2012.

Okoro, Dike. "Ojaide Sings *The Tale of the Harmattan* from Cape Town": *Africanwriter.com*.

Available at,www.aftricanwriter.comojaide-sings-the-tale-of-the-hartmann-from-cape-town/

Saro-Wiwa, Ken. *Genocide in Nigeria: The Ogoni Tragedy.* Saros International, 1992.

Tcheuyap, Alexis. "Entre films romans: Des réécriturestextuellesenAfrique Francophone."

Ph.D. Diss., Queen's University (Canada), 2001

Udje Aesthetics in Tanure Ojaide's Poetry

Adetayo Alabi

Tanure Ojaide is typically classified as a member of the second generation of African writers: positioned directly after the generation of Christopher Okigbo, Chinua Achebe, Wole Soyinka, and J. P. Clark. This second generation which includes others like Niyi Osundare and Harry Garuba , particularly in relation to poetry, reacts to the obscure and highly introspective writing of the first generation. Chinweizu, Onwuchekwa Jemie, and Ihechukwu Madubuke produced a biting criticism of the poetry of Soyinka's generation in *Toward the Decolonization of African Literature*. One of the major ways in which Ojaide's generation differs from Soyinka's is the prevalent use of orality, indigenous images, symbols, and traditions in their writings. As FunsoAiyejina argues in one of his seminal works, entitled "Recent Nigerian Poetry in English: A Critical Survey," that the newer poets started writing "accessible and socially anchored poetry" (25) within the framework of what he also calls the "alter/native tradition" in another essay entitled "Recent Nigerian Poetry in English: An Alter/Native Tradition." Aiyejina describes Ojaide in "Recent Nigerian Poetry in English: A Critical Survey" as a "neo-traditionalist" who "empathises with the downtrodden and employs a poetic style ... derived from an indigenous poetics" (33). Aiyejina argues further that Ojaide's "poetry is marked by the generous presence of sonorous phrases, parables and rituals and the absence of the obscure. He uses traditional forms to achieve poetic validity, intensity, and relevance" (33). The foundation of Ojaide's indigenous poetics, validity, and intensity is the traditional Urhobo Udje satirical tradition and this is the focus of this essay.

G. G. Darah, an Udje scholar, acknowledges the importance of Udje in Tanure Ojaide's works and he promoted the genre in his book entitled *Battles of Songs: Udje Tradition of the Urhobo* (vi and 98). He also acknowledges J. P. Clark's pioneering work on the genre. Ojaide in his own book on Udje also recognizes the works of both Clark and Darah in the Udje tradition. Darah asserts in his book that Udje "as an artistic tradition had three aspects, namely, dance, poetry, and music. The point of emphasis in the study is inter-group rivalry relationship (*omesuo*) amongst the practitioners. This relationship was expressed in the following ways: the division of the communities or performance troupes into opposing pairs, the intention and wordings of the songs, and public performances at dance-song festivals. Indeed, the whole business of Udje was conducted as a kind of verbal warfare, battles of songs in which each participating group attempted to *sing its rival to a fall*" (Darah vii).

According to Tanure Ojaide (in *Poetry, Performance, and Art: Udje Dance Songs of the Urhobo People*),

Udje is a unique type of Urhobo dance in which rival, occasionally hostile, quarters or towns perform songs composed from often exaggerated materials about the other side on an appointed day. Udje songs are thus dance songs sung when udje is being performed. Udje is an integrative performance that involves singing and dancing by costumed and seasoned performers. It is associated with seasonal festivals and rituals in various parts of Urhobo. (4)

Ojaide discusses the form of the Udje poem and describes it in terms of a four-part structure in his foreword to his book of poems entitled *Songs of Myself: Quartet*. The book, according to Ojaide, is deeply rooted in the indigenous African poetic tradition. The great *udje* poets first composed songs paying tribute to the god of songs, followed by songs of self-exhortation, and then songs mocking themselves before satirizing others. This collection incorporates some of these aspects of the oral poetic genre in its four-part structure. It deals with self-examination and the minstrel's alter-ego as a way of attempting to know himself. So, there is self-mockery that justifies mocking others. The four parts of the collection are: 'Pulling the Thread of the Loom,' 'Songs of Myself,' 'Songs of the Homeland Warrior,' and 'Secret Love and Other Poems.'(6)

Ojaide continues:

In the first quartet, the poet assumes the persona of an old man who has experienced much over time and shares his experience of life with others. It ends with advice to youths and speaks on how life has to do with multitasking. In the second quartet, the minstrel presents a persona who mocks himself and in doing so tells us about the society he lives in and its penchant for singling out individuals for criticism. Thus, the poet and his society are simultaneously interrogated in their respective roles in private and public spheres. The third quartet, "Songs of the Homeland Warrior," has to do with the poet's Niger Delta experience. While the persona laments ecological and environmental damage and changes, he criticizes not only outsiders that have caused damage but also his people's representatives. The concluding quartet, "Secret Love and Other Poems," starts with an emblematic poem and goes on to deal with the poet's inner wanderings and thoughts about life. This section also features a variety of poems. The format of the four-part structure affords the poet the opportunity to deal with personal and public experiences in a closely related fashion. These poems have engaged the poet for more than five years (6).

In the four parts of Ojaide's book, following the Udje quartet, Ojaide places different poems in four groups that can serve as tribute to the ancestors and the muse; panegyric or self-adulating poems; auto/biographical satire; and bio/communal/global satire. The categories are fairly fluid in Ojaide's categorization such that some poems fit in more than one area. This is crucial because Ojaide's notation about the "bio" goes beyond the individual poet to include his immediate community and the globe at large. For example, his Foreword to the book is signed identifying two locations, Nigeria and the US. This shows clearly that the subject matter in the poem and Ojaide's poetic manifestos in the text go beyond the individual to the local and to the global.

Part 1 of the collection of poems subtitled "Pulling the Thread of the Loom" deals with the traditional homage that the great Udje poets sing to honor their predecessors and literally open the poet's mouth so that he or she can sing and perform unhindered. This is the section where Ojaide shares his experiences to mobilize the youths against injustices in the Delta. The section starts with a song and places another song toward its end. The starting song entitled "Gently" (15) and the concluding song entitled "For Youths" (60) illustrate the song tradition of the genre. The principal poetic and song narrative strategy is call and response. This shows the presence and involvement of both the performer and the audience. The opening song also serves as the invocation to situate the poet as he starts his song. The call that starts the song-poem is "Dede-e dede-e" and the response is "Gently and steadily the old man pulls the thread of the loom." The old man obviously has to pull the thread gently to be able to weave a successful tapestry of images. Ojaide describes his opening line in the note to the poem as "onomatopoeic expression of 'gently' in the Urhobo language" (15). From gently and steadily pulling the words, the poet starts to introduce the themes of the poem. Irony and paradox are two of the major figures of speech the poet uses to introduce his subject matter and to involve the audience in the performance of the day as in the following example: "He limps his way through the rugged terrain that stretches before him / but outpaces strides of those without age or other kinds of challenges." Another example of irony is in the relationship between cock crow and sunrise: "More than thrice, and accompanied by its kind, the cock crows at dawn / but only once does the cheerful but taciturn sun rise to wake up the world" (15). The song toward the end of the section entitled "For Youths" is a warrior song and rallying call to mobilize the youths to the realities of their society and to be resistant to societal inhumanity. The call is Omo Okogbe which could be a reference to a child in Okogbe a village in Ahoada West in Rivers State, but it is more plausible to interpret the song as a battle cry and mobilization strategy. The response is Okogbe and this is repeated throughout the poem as the poet depicts the image of a warrior "whose grandfather had been a warrior chief" ready to struggle, fight, and lead a resistance movement. Unfortunately, the warrior is not prepared for the fight ahead so "he lost his life." (60). The consequence is that "Now a song mocks the youth rushing in to challenge/those already out in the field or coming in with tight lips" (61). This poem raises the issue of the youthful warriors' preparedness for battle and the warning that the struggle could be lost if the youth was not prepared for the fight ahead. This is also reminiscent of the historical Biafra war in Nigeria when, Christopher Okigbo, one of Africa's most gifted poets joined the Biafra armed forces and lost his life in battle.

Paying obeisance is a major theme of this section and this is represented in poems like: "No Hunger" (16) and "Questing" (20). The poet needs to pay his dues to his progenitors so that they can open the way for him and he can sing well. As the poet puts it in "No hunger," "The minstrel suffers no hunger/ in the famine of songs. "Aridon's favorite suffers no hunger / in the famine of songs" (16). "The god of songs suffers no hunger / in the famine of ardent worshippers" (17). Aridon, according to the poet's note is the "god of memory and song / poetry among the Urhobo people" (17).

Ojaide also addresses globalization and social injustice themes in this section in poems like "After Reading King Leopold's Ghost" (45), "Masika" (for rape victims of Congo DR) (47), "Medellin Testament" (on Columbia and Bolivar) (49), and "For the Drowned, at Lampedusa" (for African immigrants that drowned in Italy) (62). "After Reading King Leopold's Ghost" focuses on the injustices meted out to the Congolese during the colonization of the country by King Leopold of Belgium. The poem underscores the racial brutality of colonialism and claims that "All the profits from ivory and rubber / that maimed or killed hundreds of thousands / the Old king threw into procuring dresses / for a teenage prostitute as a total paramour" (45) and "all the severed hands and cracked skulls, all the tears / of wood and folks for the love of a teenage prostitute" (46). Ojaide's focus here is the type that Joseph Conrad ignores in *Heart of Darkness* that he sets in the Congo and the type that Chinua Achebe focuses on in "An Image of Africa: Racism in Joseph Conrad's *Heart of Darkness."*

Some of the poems are also autobiographical. "Effurun Market" (51) details the poet's visit to the market and raises issue of tradition and modernity, colonial arrogance and transgression against the logic of the market, and other things that happen in the market beyond trading. "Okpara Night" (53) recalls the poet's experiences visiting Okpara waterside in Delta State and foregrounds diaspora and exile consciousness in "Spirit" (57) that is dedicated to Chimalum Nwankwo (a colleague of the poet nicknamed "Spirit"). "The Road to Kilifi" (65) compares the Kilifi Kenyan coastal town with the landscape of the Delta and expresses his concerns about "cross-border raids" (64).

Section 2 of the quartet is subtitled "Songs of Myself." This is where the poet satirizes himself so that he can satirize others. In "Mother Hen" (71), the poet compares his muse to mother hen; and in "Heartbreaks" (72), he claims that without his experiences, he won't be here today. This is one of the poems where he uses anaphora so well for communication. In the title poem, "Song of Myself" (73 and 74), the poet is disillusioned and upset because the muse or lover doubts his sincerity. The poet swears by the pen literally in "He Swears by the Pen" (75) and he invokes Wole Soyinka and Chinua Achebe and their writings on the significance of the pen, virtue and vice. The most profound satire on the poet are in poems like "If the Poet Were the Butt of His Own Songs" (77) and "To the New Wordsmiths" (78-79). In "If the Poet Were the Butt of His Own Songs," the poet uses the rhetorical questioning strategy to thematize the fate of the poet if satirized: "If the popular poet were the butt of his own songs / how sharp would he hone his words to wound himself ...and if the famous composer were the butt of his own songs / what consideration would give a sharper edge to laughter?" (77). "To the New Wordsmiths" is a satire on new and inexperienced poets calling them "baby imbongis" from the South African Izibongo praise tradition and referring to them as "under-ripened fruits / plucked there to upstage those waiting for fruits to fall." He uses irony to criticize the poets further by comparing them to the child who calls himself a man but asks "a bearded one to crack the walnut for him." (78). He also calls them "new griots in ponds [but] behave as if in an ocean" (78). In the poem entitled "Family Counselor" (85), the poet autobiographically takes the position of the first born in the family and identifies an irony in the role of the first born who is required by the mother to counsel the younger ones for the offenses he commits. He ends the poem by asking rhetorically "how the goat will condemn its kind, / or disrobe myself of priesthood and lose face!" "Wayo Man" (87) presents the poet as a trickster and this is full of personal criticism in the Udje tradition of self-criticism to get the license to criticize others. He continues the representation of the poet as a trickster in "I Am so Predictable" (93) and reveals some autobiographical elements, including efforts to hide his gender as a child to prevent harm against him: "I am so predictable / I was born a girl / it took five years for my father's / family to discover I am male" (94). "Acquittal" (89) is also about self-criticism. "Self-defense" (91) is where he defends the poet for not being a warrior but still useful to the society:

> They say I am the loafer, the stay-at-home one
> and everybody smacks me with terrible insults!
> When the warrior chief's home caught fire in his absence
> I spotted it and alerted folks to stop the savage blaze;
>
> when the wealthy farmer's mother took ill and collapsed
> I, the reviled loafer, the stay-at-home one, revived her (91)

He continues:

> They say I haven't the bile it takes in the liver
> to kill a snake not to talk of catching snakefish,
>
> they say I am like rock salt used in preparing dishes
> and would melt and so cannot fish or farm in the rain
>
> but I am sent on errands, the town-crier of every season.
> I composed the chant that makes leopards of warriors;
>
> in days of Biafra I spotted camouflaged saboteurs
> before military intelligence recovered from rape orgies.
>
> I compose lethal songs that at every *udje* festival
> destroy boastful rivals and make us invincible warriors;
>
> of course our performers always take the credit for them
> as those like me everywheredispossessed and silenced (91)

From these poems on self-criticism, the poet goes on to criticize others like the Nigerian National Assembly in "The New Lotus Eaters" (105) and satirizes those who say his child is ugly in "They Say My Child is Ugly Like a Goat" (107).

Section 3, subtitled "Songs of the Homeland Warrior," is where the poet criticizes the ecological destruction and social injustice in his homeland. The poem entitled "Come and Spend a Day with Me" (128) is the poet's invitation to the reader to come on the journey to the delta to see what's going on there. The poet declares: "come and experience the life we live / and see for yourself the rigors we bear / and tell others the tale of our blues" (128). The poet focuses on naming, discourse, and power to control and shape opinions in the Foucauldian tradition in "If Those They Called Militants" (112). The poet claims that it is misnaming to call them militants because they are fighting for their rights. If the table turned and

> If those called militants had *The New York Times* or *The Times of London*
> they would call their detractors unprintable names
> ....
> if the homeland warriors called militants
> had their own CNN and Aljazeera
> they would call their robbers monsters

they would ask nations
why they fought for independence
from occupiers of their lands (112)

He continues this criticism of the abusers and claims they would have fought harder if they had an inheritance in the defiled communities "If They Had Their Gods Here." The poetic devices of choice here are anaphora, piling, and association. Here is an excerpt from the poem:

If they had their gods here
if they buried their ancestors here
if their totem pet roamed here
if their muse drank from here
if their arts were inspired by this landscape
if they raised their children in this community
if they made their living from this soul and water
if they exercised their leisure here
If this land affirmed their humanity
....
they would battle even harder to victory (113)

The criticism of the society (as poachers and developers pillage the environment) is seen in "Can I Still Call from the River Nun?" (114-115). In "Don't Follow the Palm Wine Tapper's Course," the poet criticizes Odjoboro who built a canoe with soft wood instead of sturdy wood, but unfortunately today, what we have are those who cannot even find wood anymore because of deforestation and ecological damage in the society (116). Military destruction of the Delta is focused on in "In the Theater of War" (136) where the poet criticizes the incessant military raids of the region. The result of the destruction is that the territory becomes "an expanse of rubble." The port is "peopled with ghosts" and the poet asks rhetorically whether anyone "can tell blood from oil sludge" (136). The environment becomes a "pool of blood" and "a wasteland" that is "fueled by oil and gas" (136).

The theme of ecological exploitation continues in "In the Omoja River" (117) and that of environmental pollution in "Much of the Year Wet" (118 - 119). Gas flare and environmental destruction are the poet's concerns in "At Eruemukohwarien" (121). He addresses environmental degradation in "The Zestful Fingers Lost its Fine Fingers" (122) and focuses on the absent fish in "The Multitude of Fish" (124). The poet now claims in "Only in His Memory" (120) that the green, bucolic, and peaceful past is only in memory because of the destruction caused by oil wells: "Only in memory / thrive the affluent residents of the wetlands ... Only in his memory / the exuberance of his irrecoverable youth .... Now he carries scars of burns / watches his companions afflicted with toxic fumes" (120). The poet's nostalgia is also the focus of "I Pass the Same Roads" (126) that others like the Bekederemo (Clarks in Kiagbodo in Delta State—author's note) passed but so much has changed because of the work of the multinational oil companies in destroying the land. The poet now criticizes his people for not standing up for their rights as much as they should do in "If I Were to Ask My People" (132) and he uses Pidgin to comment on the society's misplaced priorities in "We Dey Chop Akara Dey Go" (133). The poet claims that the people are eating and making merry instead of demanding for a total overhaul of their society: "We dey chop akara dey go / if moin-moin no dey ... in place of clean rivers / Shell dey build boreholes ...." (133). The use of Pidgin to comment on the people's complacency here is significant because it is one of the languages most commonly used and accessible in the region. It also suggests that the society in question is multilingual.

Section 4 of the quartet is subtitled "Secret Love and Other Poems." The first poem of this section entitled "The Painting Suite" celebrates a painting the poet got as a gift in the middle of an ecological disaster (142). The poet implicitly compares the beauty of the painting with the destruction of the environment in his homeland. The poem is in four parts like the Udje quartet. The poem celebrates the unnamed landscape in part 1. "Beautiful Figure, Beautiful Landscape," the poet calls it (142). It is "a congress on a canvas, / a reunion of birds at a magic stream of colors" (142). In part 2, the poet calls the painter "a magician delivering colors / and I seek currents to whet my songs" (143). The poet is so impressed with the painting that he "will muster the minstrel's craft of magic / to smother the painting with praise-chants" (144). The painting is "exhilarating beauty" in part 3 (144) and in part 4 it is "exceptional glamor" (145). The poet discusses contradictory encounters between poet and muse in "In Contest" (150) and uses irony to describe a society without wars and mass destruction in "For the Muse of Peace" (152). Although "For the Muse of Peace" celebrates peace and peaceful co-existence, the reality of the society is the sub text of war and destruction.

"(Re) visitation" dwells on the autobiographical theme of a previous visit to a Warri Street where, forty years before, Ojaide saw a schoolgirl give her lunch money to a beggar; but during this new visit or revisit, things are so bad that he sees several beggars with pans in hand. He remembers the girl who gave money to the beggar and knows "what to do as others pass them by" (160). "In a Tent Room" (168) is also autobiographical and about a visit to Kilifi in coastal

Kenya. The poet comments on the beauty of the landscape and the hospitality of those he met. Unlike "(Re) visitation" and "In a Tent Room" that are autobiographical, "Homage: To My Friend's Father's" is biographical. It is about the poet's friend's father and his struggle for education and resources in a polygamous home. The poet comments on art and masks in "Masks" (170-172) and stresses how people tell stories through masks. The masks "show the beauty that does not fade" and they "remind us of what not to forget." (169). The poem takes an autobiographical tone when the poet describes himself as a mask "nailed to outlast the home" and "a sensational figure before graying air" and "now a mask on the painted wall" (170).

The poet examines societal hypocrisy after the powerful loses his or her position. In this case, the focus is on how the society reacts after a senator dies in "Death of a Senator" (163). There is premonition of the senator's death as bees assemble in his home and later in Abuja the seat of power after they have been chased from his home with fire. Death ultimately silences the assertive senator. While some praise him, others criticize him. The irony of the society lies in the fact that people start to clamor for the senator's position even before the burial: "the colleagues begin / to fight for the vacated money-doubling seat / and boast in orgies of senator-in-waiting; / they sow fire seeds for wandering spirits" (164). The poem also satirizes how much the Nigerian society focuses on power and the wealth that accrues to many political office holders.

In "Of Humidity and Hydration" (173), the poet comments on climate change and ineffective political leadership. The heat from the sun is so overwhelming that it will "drive someone crazy" (173). He compares the sun to the unreachable nation's president: "the sun is the nation's president the *oga* at the top / it lives in Aso Rock in a planet beyond reach" (173). The mood of the sun is unpredictable, just like that of the nation's leader who is distant until the campaigns. According to the poet, "My country is an arthritic nation with all the resources / but disabled in ways too daunting to spring out of damnation— / blame it on humidity for not tapping sense out of big brains; / blame Providence for giving wealth to who cannot manage it!" (175).

In the same section, "Next to God" is about experiences of dilemmas and solutions (176). That is why a patient will consider his or her doctor as next to God. The section ends with "Waiting" (177) that is in continuity and "For the New Year" that is on cyclic continuity, beginnings and endings. Perhaps the most humorous poem in the whole text is "Let Them Die for Arsenal" (165) where Ojaide returns to the theme of globalization and how the European football leagues are exported to the rest of the world and particularly embraced by Nigerian football fans. The epigraph to the poem is by a Nigerian fan who said he was ready to die for Arsenal, during a competition between Arsenal and Hull City on May 17, 2014, at a time when Nigeria was reeling with the shock and embarrassment of the kidnapped Chibok girls. There are so many local causes to fight and die for and so many local problems listed in the poem like armed robbery, rape, war, police and soldiers, religion, witchcraft, snakebite, motor crash, heart attack, etc. (165-166), but the fan is only prepared to die for an English club. Ojaide repeats the line "Let them die for Arsenal" throughout the poem for emphasis and he puns the fan's statement to show the irony in how people approve of and dwell on what is foreign while their own domestic issues and potential suffer. The poet uses anaphora and repetition humorously to satirize those who want to die for Arsenal. He writes:

> Let them die for Arsenal
> and millions more for Chelsea, Manchu [sic], and Real Madrid
> ....

You don't die for many causes
you don't die for Arsenal and still die for Nigeria
you die for only one cause
you don't die for Arsenal and still bring back our stolen children
there is only one death
die for Arsenal and you are gone as a person
you have only one life
throw it away for Arsenal and desecrate your homeland.
die for Arsenal.

Die for Arsenal, my king of fools
die for Arsenal, my retarded brother
die for Arsenal, my homeless relative
die for Arsenal whose body will be carcass for vultures
die for Arsenal, whose body won't be buried in England
die for Arsenal, stray rabid dog
die for Arsenal, my compatriot
die for Arsenal who will not die for God
let them all die for Arsenal.

In conclusion, Udje poetry is still alive and practiced in many parts of the delta in Nigeria and in many other areas Urhobo people have migrated to, especially within Nigeria. Both traditionally and contemporarily, the Udje genre is used for entertainment, criticism, exercise, creativity, and competitiveness. Ojaide comments on the traditional use of the genre and argues that its satirical element allows the society to critique vices and criminals since there were no prisons for criminals in the traditional society. As he argues in *Poetry, Performance, and Art*, "major crimes were punished either by selling the criminal into servitude or by executing him. Minor crimes were, however, punished by satire. The songs strongly assail what the traditional society regards as vices: laziness, vanity, wretchedness, miserliness, flirtation, adultery, prostitution, wickedness, and greed. Occasionally, there are blatant lampoons as when barrenness, ugliness, and other natural deformities of a person are sung. The singers want what they consider to be positive norms of the society to be upheld. Thus central to the concept of Udje dance songs are the principles of correction and deterrence through punishment with 'wounding' words" (Ojaide, *Poetry* 4). What is most important to the people and Udje practitioners, therefore, is to correct and prevent bad behavior through the songs. This is also what Ojaide does with the genre: to entertain, to criticize for improvement and social justice, and to prevent the society from getting worse even as it continues its encounter with modernity and globalization.

Contemporarily, the Udje genre serves two additional functions. Ojaide asserts that the "songs serve as a lesson to today's journalists and publishers of tabloids" not just to make up stories without any truths because the traditional genre and society had "sanctions against falsehoods as well as lampoons against natural defects. Exaggerated as the content of some of the songs may be, there is always some element of truth that provokes the composition" (*Poetry* 5). Another contemporary relevance of the genre is how Ojaide and other scholars have brought it to modernity and a kind of globalization coming from Africa to the rest of the world. Ojaide through the genre showcases traditional African culture and civilization as represented by the Urhobo and makes it clear to the world that the tradition is as sophisticated as any satirical genre in the world. As Ojaide puts it, the "experience of foreign / western and written African literatures compelled me to examine what my people have as literature. Deducting from my experience and training, I have no doubt that *Udje* dance songs are some of the most poetic of traditional African songs I have ever examined. Therefore, they deserve to be considered alongside the Akan and Ewe dirges; Yoruba *Ijala*, *Oriki* and divination poems; and Xhosa and Xulu *Izibongo*" (*Poetry* 5). Along with promoting African culture and countering racism with African traditions, Ojaide recalls that a poignant experience that fuels his work in the Ujde tradition came in 1984 at the International Writing Program at the University of Iowa when Frederic Will suggested that some languages were not able to produce great literature. Ojaide dismissed Frederic Will's claim "as Western arrogance that considers its written literature to be the only worthy literature and ignores the vast oral literature in Africa and elsewhere in the world" and hopes that his "research will allow critics to judge whether Urhobo literature, as exemplified by *Udje* dance songs, is good or worthwhile in the context of current trends in the field" (*Poetry* 7).

Works Cited

Achebe, Chinua. "An Image of Africa: Racism in Conrad's *Heart of Darkness*." *Hopes and Impediments: Selected Essays 1965–1987*. Heinemann, 1988, 1–13.

Aiyejina, Funso. "Recent Nigerian Poetry in English: A Critical Survey." *Kunapipi* IX:2 (1987): 24-36.

—. "Recent Nigerian Poetry in English: An Alter-Native Tradition." In Ed. Ogunbiyi, Yemi. *Perspectives on Nigerian Literature 1700 to the Present*. Volume 1. Guardian Books Nigeria Limited, 1988, 112–28.

Alabi, Adetayo. "Introduction: Africa in a Global Age." *The Global South* 2.2 (Fall 2008):1-9.

—. "Tanure Ojaide and The Udje Quartet: Song, Satire, Social Justice,and Globalization,"
delivered at the 16th Annual Africana StudiesSymposium, University of North Carolina at   Charlotte, February 22-23,2018.

—. *Telling Our Stories: Continuities and Divergences in Black Autobiographies*

—. "The Auto/biographical Images of Africa in Udje Poetry," delivered at the African Literature
Association 35th Annual Meeting and Conference, University of Vermont, Burlington, VT, April 15-19, 2009.

—. "The Role of Udje in Tanure Ojaide's Poetry," delivered at the Ojaide at 70

Symposium, Kwara State University Conference Center, Ilorin, July 9, 2018.

—. "Udje Aesthetics in Tanure Ojaide's Poetry," delivered at the 12th Conference of the International Society for the Oral Literatures of Africa (ISOLA), University of Ibadan, Nigeria, July 10-12, 2018.

Chinweizu, Onwuchekwa Jemie, and Ihechukwu Madubuke *Towards the Decolonization of African Literature*. Fourth Dimension, 1980.

Clark, J.P. "Poetry of the Urhobo Dance Udje." *Nigeria Magazine* 87 (1965): 282-287.

Conrad, Joseph. *Heart of Darkness*. Ed. Paul B. Armstrong. 4th Edition. (Norton Critical Edition). W.W. Norton and Company, 2006.

Darah, G.G. "Aesthetics of Udje Performance Event at Agbara." *Agufon: A Journal of the Arts and Architecture*, 2000 (10-15).

—. Aesthetics Socialization of Youth Through Dance and Music in Urhobo Society." Odu 28
(July 1985): 45-56.

—. *Battle of Songs: Udje Tradition of the Urhobo*. Malthouse Press Limited, 2005

—. "Dance as an Agent of Social Mobilization in Urhobo." *Nigeria Magazine* 54.1 (1986): 20-35.

—. Dramatic Presentation in Udje Dance Performance of the Urhobo. *Drama and Theatre in Nigeria* 1991, 504-516.

Finnegan, Ruth. *Oral Literature in Africa*. Oxford University Press, 1970.

Foucault, Michel. "The Order of Discourse" (1970). *Untying the Text*. Ed. Robert Young.

Routledge and Kegan Paul, 1981. 48–78.

Ojaide, Tanure. *Poetry, Performance, and Art: Udje Dance Songs of the Urhobo People*.
North Carolina Academic Press, 2003.

—. *Songs of Myself: Quartet*. Kraft Books Limited, 2015.

—. *Theorizing African Oral Poetic Performance and Aesthetics: Udje Dance Songs of the Urhobo People*. Africa World Press, 2009.

Okpewho, Isidore. *African Oral Literature: Background, Character, and Continuity.* Indiana University Press, 1992.

Usanga, Kufre. "Orature and Eco-Engagement in Tanure Ojaide's *Songs of Myself*."

International Journal of Humanities and Cultural Studies 4.4 (2018) 245-257.

Signs, Significations and Functions:

A Semiotic Approach to Tanure Ojaide's *Delta Blues and Home Songs*

Psalms Emeka Chinaka & Okwudiri Anasiudu

Introduction

Tanure Ojaide's poetic vision, which draws substantially from eco-aesthetics and the cultural resource of the Niger Delta such as the Udje oral / traditional poetry of the Urhobo, can be effectively interpreted through signs. These signs have intricate signifying patterns with varied communicative functions which are complex and inversed. The term communicative, according to John Fiske, is the ability of signs to "refer to something other than themselves" (1). In Ojaide's poetry, certain signs are deployed in order to refer to the environmental despoliation and economic deprivation of the people of the Niger Delta.

Ojaide's semiotic repertoires have something in common in its special terms and language. On its part, language itself is an unstable phenomenon. Paul Cobley is of the view that language is open to several definitions (5). Within the semantic schema of semiotics, Charles Bressler explains that language is a sign, "a system…that conveys meaning" (87). Other scholars, like Best and Kellner view language as "differing signifiers that produce meaning" (19). Ojaide's poetic enterprise relies heavily on language or signs which are interconnected with other signs in his poems. In other words, signs do not occur "in isolation" (Chandler 2), as they are evaluated in relation to a context and within the frame of Mailloux's "interpretive conventions as rules for correct interpretation" (124).

One of the ways by which the signs in Ojaide's poetry assume meaning is through annexation. Annexation is the ability of an image to "mime what it represents" (Mbembe 142). It implies thus: to appropriate, to assume a new meaning which is not evident in the lexical surface realization. It also engenders a form of ambiguity which William Empson calls a "second type of ambiguity" (48). This kind of ambiguity occurs when two or more meanings are resolved into one, a kind of arbitrariness which negotiates a nexus between the signifier and the signified. For example, the oil leitmotif in Ojaide's poetry is an example of annexation, in terms of the re-presentation of economic marginalization, environmental degradation, and violence in the Niger Delta. It is also noteworthy that semantic annexation is a peculiar signifying strategy in poetry, generally.

It is wrong to assume that one knows what a particular sign presupposes or entails outside a context. Following the Saussurean model, a signifier and signified share an arbitrary relation, but within the systemic orientation, the signifier serves an ideational meta-function which is context bound and sensitive. One of the tasks of this work is to articulate a solution to the problem of signs, signification and function. Therefore, the premise of this work is to explain that there are three meaning assigners or ways of assigning meaning to a sign. The first is the meaning a sign assumes by the principle of convention, that is, a generally accepted meaning for a sign by a community of sign users. For example, it is generally a tacit agreement that the stars and the crescent moon is a signifier for Islam. Another example is the offering of a kolanut to a guest in Igbo land, which signals acceptance.

The second way of assigning meaning to a sign is for a poet to force meaning into a sign in a poem in terms of the use of private images and symbols. This kind of private use of images are common to poets like T. S Eliot in his "Waste Land;" even Christopher Okigbo shares such sensibilities in his poem the "Prodigal." The third meaning assigner is the reader who reads a sign and offers a new perspective to it. However, each of the meaning assigners is dependent on the context of emergence of a sign.

Linguists have greatly advanced the study of signs; whether they are formalists or functionalists. The formalist linguists are handicapped by their inability to ascribe social meanings to a sign beyond its grammatical description. The functionalist approach on the other hand is a logical aftermath of the noticeable deficiencies of the mentalist model. However, semiotics which is a kind of functionalist approach is broad-based. This is because it blends the linguistic and extra-linguistic elements of language in sign interpretation. Its scope of signification transcends verbal and orthographic signs to embrace other issues as raised by Cobley, such as body language, music, animal communication systems, traffic signals (5). In poetry as a genre, the deployment of the semiotic system of signs is a vital part of its communication function and strategy. This is essentially because of its socio-functional bearing, which Ikenna Kamalu sees as a "social and cultural context" (73) or what Terry Eagleton calls "cultural and historical conventions" (84). Apart from the sociological thrust of sign in poetry, a sign also focalizes or calls attention to a text.

Arriving at a correct meaning or interpretation for a sign, which Eagleton calls the "process of re-reading" (89) is not an easy task, especially for poetry which is a complex, opaque and condensed form of discourse. Eagleton further notes that "the structures [of a poem] can only be perceived retrospectively… poetry activates the full body of signifier, presses the word to work to its utmost, under the intense pressure of surrounding words, and so release its richest potential" (89). Given that not every interpretation of a sign is correct, Eagleton calls attention to the first problem of signs which is the nature of their signification as they are open to multiple meaning. No sign exists in a semantic vacuum; every sign has a semantic context of emergence. Thus, if one identifies the context of emergence of any sign and situates this sign within this context, the probability of arriving at a correct interpretation of a sign may be very possible. This is particularly so for the poetic genre.

A Semiotic Reading of Selected Poems in Tanure Ojaide's *Delta Blues and Home Songs*

Ojaide's collection, *Delta Blues and Home Songs,* is made up of 51 poems of strongly accentuated lyricism, social realism, free verse, evocative pathos, and absence of a strict adherence to uniformity in its stanzaic pattern. The first part, *Delta Blues,* contains 28 poems while the second part, *Home Songs,* contains 23 poems. Each of the poems is related in terms of subject matter and focuses on the Niger Delta. Structurally, they are connected by varied semiotic forms which necessitate the cohesion and logic of the text. These signs are assigned meaning by the convention or semantic universe of the various groups like the Urhobo, Izon, Ogoni, and Kalabari which are part of the Niger Delta linguistic grouping. They constitute source area for the creative materials of Ojaide's poetry.

In the first poem, "My Drum Beats Itself," the subject matter is the emergence of an apprentice who celebrates achievement or success, hence, acknowledges the effort of a mentor. This is represented in line 1, of the first stanza: "now that my drum beats itself / I know that my dead ancestor's hand is at work." This idea of success or achievement, which it celebrates, is construed through the sign "drum." The sign "drum" is repeated in lines 6, 30 and 31. It is also a major signifier, upon which the meanings of the poem rest. This drum which beats itself could be wooden or metal, but its signification is not within its appellation as a signifier "drum" or as a syllable /d r ʌ m/. Its signification can be understood when explained within its syntagmatic or associative relationship with other sign systems of the poem like "chant" in line 12, "ear" in line 18, music in line 20. What these signs share in common is that they are of the universal set ($\sum$ = **chant, ear, music, drum**) of phonic-semiotics, such that their meanings are communicated through sounds. An example of a drum which comes to mind in the Niger Delta region is the Ikoro.

There are two perspectives to the drum as a sign system deployed in the poem. The first perspective is that the lexical item drum is generally associated with phonic components. But the reference is not just to the phonological or prosodic aspects of the drum. There is a deeper signification associated with the term "drum." The second perspective to the drum is thus connotative. It is a reference to success and achievement as a result of training and/or mentorship which the persona calls "another music that fills the air which cannot be heard without effort" (line 21). Humans can hear the sound of a drum by virtue of the human physiological component of an ear, but not everyone can hear a sound from the drum which beats itself. This is because it is impossible for a drum to beat itself. It appears surreal; more like magic. It therefore suggests that the poet is not calling attention to the usual meaning associated with drum or the sound it makes, but to another meaning associated with the drum. What the "drum" beating itself implies is that one's achievements or success speaks for itself. For the persona, this is an achievement which comes after series of training and learning, hence the need for self-adulation. This further corroborates the proposition that the drum is not just a drum but a symbol of achievement, hard work, and success; and it does not come to everyone without efforts. The above explanation reveals the irony of signs as contrastive to their signified. In the drum beating itself, there is also a wisdom that is communicated. This is a wisdom which explains how success is achieved. The persona ascribes the reason for success to the role of a "mentor" who wants him to succeed.

There are other functions of the sign "drum" within its linguistic context as a tool for foregrounding, through deviation. The drum is imbued with animate qualities, such as the capacity to initiate action which is a form of lexico-semantic deviation. This kind of deviation occurs in other poems in the collection. For example: "streets echo with wails" in line 36 of "Wails," "a column of helmet-dressed Anthills marched through his youth" in line 6 of "Journeying," "history will take its revenge" in line 28 of "On Solidarity March" and "the ironwood that torments the executive axe" in line 16 of the "Prisoner." The purpose of such pattern of arrangement, where certain signs are made to come alive, is to call attention to the meaning they refer to. These inanimate entities are imbued with life. Ironically, humans assume that such things do not have a life of their own, which is logically correct. Nevertheless, there are cultural principles that such sign systems, used by the poet, attempt to communicate. The deviations as demonstrated in these poems are consciously created to allegorize human life, human attributes and nature. Their significations are assigned to them by the convention of their context of emergence. Nevertheless, within another context of emergence their signification may change entirely.

Instances where signs serve specific functions are evident in the title-poem: "Delta Blues." The sign system is deployed to serve a descriptive function. The signs create an image of the ecological state of the Niger Delta. Particularly, this descriptive function is realized through the use of eco-semiotic signs, such as salt, fish, plants, birds, rivers, and mangrove. This kind of interpretation is realized by observing how the signs relate and share sameness in a context. In this case, the meaning of such signs is assigned by the reader, dependent on the reader's adroitness, and knowledge of the interpretive conventions of the context of emergence of a given sign as exemplified in the following lines:

The **rivers are dark-veined**
A course of perennial draughts
This **home of salt and fish**
Stilted in mangroves, market barter,
This **home of plants and birds**
North or south of this **paradise**.

Another function of signs is the capacity to enable a text or a poem to cohere or stick together as a unified whole. A careful observation of a sign matrix unveils a syntagmatic arrangement which functions as a cohesive device. It imbues a poem with an organic architecture and logic of form. This is evident below:

The   **rivers**   are dark-veined

A course of perennial draughts

This **home of   salt   and   fish**

Stilted in mangroves, market barter,

This **home of   plants   and   birds**

   North or south of this   **paradise**

The highlighted lexical items are key operators of the above poem which enable the poem to have coherence. The absence of the lexical items will affect the overall meaning the poem intends to communicate. "Home of salt and fish" is in paradigmatic relation with "home of plant and birds," as they are close substitutes which point to the beauty and rich fauna of the Niger Delta. The poem depicts the Niger Delta as a beautiful place, a paradise.

The function of signs as cohesive devices is also evident in the poem "Odebala." This is achieved through the second person pronominal "he" which is deployed with other terms like "his," where they serve as anaphoric reference to Odebala the antecedent in the poem. In terms of information structure, the function of the pronominal signs "he" and "his," in the poem, refer to the previous information given at the opening of the poem, Odebala.

Odebala   boasts he is rich,

I only hope   knows what wealth provides!

Odebala swaggers, puffs out   shoulders

Because   daydreams he's rich.

We know   inherited debts from   father

And   hands are neither strong nor fortunate.

In another instance, cohesion is further shown. This is evident in Ojaide's "Sleeping in a Makeshift Grave." The lexical items "she," a pronominal, is deployed as a signification for the nation Nigeria. Particular attention should also be given to the gender it reflects, as Nigeria is portrayed or described as a female capable of procreation. The highlighted words in the excerpt below indicate this:

Nigeria sleeps in a makeshift grave.
If **she** wakes with stars as **her** eyes,
The next world will be brighter for me and compatriots.
A gunful of **children** broke the tetrarch's legs
& the elephant that once pulled the forest along for a path has fallen-
Can **she** get up before **she's** covered for dead?

In "When Green Was the Lingua Franca," one needs to appreciate the sign assemblage of ecological symbols to call attention to the environmental degradation which characterizes the Niger Delta geo-space which was once described as a paradise. The sign – "green" - ordinarily signifies colour, but at the secondary signification it means vegetation, ecology. Its super-ordinate includes: "fish" in line 10, "earth-worm" in line 12, "water, and cotton tree" in line 29. These sign systems trigger a feeling of remembrance, of the childhood life or existence of the persona. It is this life or existence that the persona reminisces as "My childhood stretched / one unbroken park, / teeming with life. / in the forest green was / the lingua franca with many dialects" line 1-6. Ironically, this existence seems to have disappeared due to ecological poachers. This is evident in the 5th stanza as other events within the poem affect the greenery, especially the activities of Shell. This is succinctly captured, in lines

63 to 67, as "Ethiope waterfront / [is] wiped out by prospectors / so many trees beheaded / and streams mortally poisoned / in the name of jobs and wealth!" Thus, beyond the primary signification of a sign, in terms of the colour green, another signification for green within the context of Ojaide's poetic vision is life, fertility, trees, and ecology. Human activities disrupt the balance of nature as shown in the poetic universe of Ojaide, thus resulting to "desert-advancing land" in line 72 of the said poem. The situation is also reflected in the poem "Seasons" where "the water sustained colouring from oil slick" (line 2). This unique deployment of sign is profound as it depicts Ojaide's commitment towards ecological activism.

A metaphorical rendering of the effect of ecological damage is demonstrated in the 6th line of "Seasons" which states: "if you took fins from a fish, would it still be fish?" This rhetorical question is couched in the interrogative mood and it foregrounds the main thrust and tenor of discourse of Niger Delta literature which revolves around the politics of oil. The sign "fish" is an aquatic entity which, within its secondary signification, symbolizes the Niger Delta people who are defined in relation to water-bodies. A pollution of the water-body, via oil exploration, is likened to taking the fins away from a fish. The consequence is that the fish is handicapped and helpless.

Another sign which signifies the menace of power in the Niger Delta is **a boa constrictor** in "Wail," lines 34-35: "for Nigeria is a boa-constrictor in the world map, as it devours its offspring's." This is a possible reference to how the type of political system practiced in Nigeria took the lives of two notable Niger Deltans: Isaac Boro and Ken Saro-Wiwa. Other poems like "Sleeping in a Makeshift Grave" and "Elegy for Nine Warriors" recount the threnodies of pain, and ultimate sacrifice paid by members of the resistance led by Saro-Wiwa and eight other Ogoni indigenes who were killed.

Conclusion

Ojaide's poetry is a conundrum of signs of various degrees. Ojaide's poetry draws heavily from ecological signs in terms of the various lexical items they evince such as: Mahogany, Iroko, palm trees, flowers, rivers, fish, waterways, and birds. These signs reflect Ojaide's eco-semiotic repertoire. Other modes of sign system deployed in Ojaide's poetry is auditory-semiotics as evident in *Delta Blues and Home Songs* (1998). These signs function as pathos and call attention to the lamentation and plight of the people in the Niger Delta.

Ojaide's deployment of sign constitutes a type of speech variety, a high diaglosia with an allegorical representation of reality. This is because it does not present reality as it is, instead it is presented in terms of irony or metaphor. This is for the purpose of communication. His signs achieve their functions by pulling down every veil from what seemingly appears normal in conventions and social reality for the purpose of communicating certain truth. Among the poets of the alter-native tradition like Niyi Osundare and Odia Ofeimun, Ojaide occupies a position as one of the poets who has been able to expand the poetic frontiers of Nigeria. This is demonstrated through the revolutionary fervency, the linguistic simplicity and the social realism of his poetic reflections.

Works Cited

Best, Steven and Kellner, Douglas. *Postmodern Theory: Critical Interrogations. The* Guilford
  Press, 1991.

Chandler, Daniel. *Semiotics the Basics*. 2nd Edition. Taylor & Francis e-library, 2007.

Cobley, Paul. "Semiosis Communication and Language". In *The Routledge Companion to Semiotics and Linguistics.* Edited by Paul Cobley, Taylor & Francis e-library, 2005.

Eagleton, Terry. *Literary Theory an Introduction.* Anniversary Edition. Blackwell Publishing, 2008.

Eco, Umberto. *Semiotics and the Philosophy of Language.* Indiana University Press, 1986.

Empson, William.. *Seven Types of Ambiguities.* Pimlico edition. Pimlico, 2004.

Fiske, John. *Introduction to Communication Study.* 2nd Edition. Taylor & Francis e-library.

Kamalu, Ikenna. *Stylistics Theory and Practice.* Kraft Books Limited, 2018.

Mailloux, Steven. "Interpretation". In *Critical Terms for Literary Study.* Edited by Frank Lentricchia and Thomas McLaughlin. University of Chicago Press, 1990.

Ojaide, Tanure. *Delta Blues and Home Song.* Kraft Books Limited, 1998.

Disillusionment and Absurdity in Tanure Ojaide's *Waiting for the Hatching of a Cockerel* and *The Beauty I Have Seen*

Mathias Iroro Orhero & Daniel George Udo

Introduction

Tanure Ojaide's poetry has attracted wide scholarship. Many critics are of the view that Ojaide is a socio-political and an eco-centric poet. While this is true, at least with reference to his previous collections of poems, his newer collection of poems are yet to attract ample critical analysis. Furthermore, critics have not critically examined the motif of disillusionment and absurdity in the poetry of Ojaide. It is this lacuna in scholarship that provides the impetus for this paper. This work is an examination of the motif of disillusionment and absurdity in the poetry of Tanure Ojaide. Two of his recent collections of poetry have been selected for this research and they are *Waiting for the Hatching of a Cockerel* (2008) and *The Beauty I Have Seen* (2010). The methodological framework for this study involves a content analysis of selected poems from the collections chosen for this research. The analysis is based on the theory and praxis of existentialism. The selected collections represent a crucial landmark in the artistic direction of Ojaide because they express deep philosophical insights on the human condition as well as the poet's vision and activism.

Tanure Ojaide was born in 1948 at Okpara-Inland in Ethiope-East Local Government Area of Delta State. He attended the University of Ibadan for his first degree and Syracuse University for his M.A. and PhD in English. His artistic career was launched with the publication of his *Children of Iroko & Other Poems* in 1973. He has about many poetry collections to his credit and he has published some short stories, novels and academic works. His poetry is an integral part of the Nigerian poetic canon and he, together with Niyi Osundare and Odia Ofeimun, is part of the well-known triad of second-generation Nigerian poets. Funso Aiyejina describes this generation as poets of the "Alter/Native" tradition (112).

Ojaide has featured in African poetry since the 1970s and his themes and techniques have changed over the years alongside the history and agitations of his people. Bassey Ude Bassey places Tanure Ojaide "in the generation of Nigerian writers after the Achebe-Clark-Okigbo-Soyinka era" (168). Commenting on the themes of Ojaide's poetry, Nesther Alu and Vashti Suwa assert that Ojaide "advances concern for the environment and the consequences" of the "unfortunate predicaments [environmental pollution] of his people" (134). Alu and Suwa's assertion is hinged on the ecological themes in Ojaide's poetry. Ojaide's collections of poems that deal with ecological themes include *Labyrinths of the Delta, The Endless Song, Daydream of Ants and Other Poems*, and *The Tale of the Harmattan* among others.

Apart from ecological themes, scholars have commented on Ojaide's socio-political themes. For example, Jide Balogun believes that "Tanure Ojaide uses poetry as a vehicle for political mediation and social control" (78). Aiyejina concludes that Ojaide is a Marxist poet (112). Some of the collections of poems that deal with socio-political issues are *The Eagle's Vision, Fate of Vultures oand Other Poems, The Blood of Peace, When It No Longer Matters Where You Live*, and others.

Ojaide is also known for the infusion of oral literary devices in his poetry. He is highly influenced by his Urhobo cultural heritage and his poetry draws from Urhobo orature. Enajite Ojaruega assessed Ojaide's use of orature in his poetry. She submits that:

... it is apparent that Ojaide uses orature to establish not only a cultural identity for his work but also organize style and form to effectively express his themes. In doing so, the poet also gives the present generation and readers an idea of their traditional heritage and how it can be used to express current and enduring thoughts and feelings. Within Ojaide's poetry, contemporary issues are sometimes reconstructed through similar episodes and events found in past Urhobo traditional oral history and folkloric heritage. (143)

Collections such as *Delta Blues and Home Songs, Invoking the Warrior Spirit, In the Kingdom of Songs, I Want to Dance and Other Poems*, among others, draw heavily from Urhobo folklore and the Udje song-poetry tradition.

Ojaide is one of the Nigerian poets residing in the United States. He is described by Moyo Okediji as "physically-dislocated" (1). Okediji further refers to Ojaide as being a "part of the Nigerian diasporic minds washed abroad during the academic brain drain of the eighties and nineties" (1). Onookome Okome identifies the exilic nature of Ojaide's poetry. His thesis is hinged on the idea that Ojaide's prolonged stay outside Nigeria has radically changed his ideology and identity so much that

Exile now seems a permanent option. It is inevitable. Ojaide, the patriot and poet, is slowly slipping into that world ... a world which Ojaide had always found incongruous to his poetic vocation. Although he still cries for home, something inside reveals that he now knows 'what it is to lose our home.' All too suddenly, we begin to notice dents on the map of the homeland that Ojaide has jealously upheld. Another kind of home is fast forming and new ideologies of life and poetic styles are forcing him to capitulate. This is the profound meaning that Ojaide's ... *When It No Longer Matters Where You Live*, a truly post-modern response to exile elicits. (12)

Abdul-Rasheed Na'Allah engages Ojaide's *I Want to Dance and Other Poems* against the background of exile and diasporan identity. To him, the collection of poems is a metaphor of "Ojaide's life journeys, from Africa to the Diaspora" (74). Using the theoretical approach of Èlàlòrò, a concept drawn from Yoruba literary criticism, Na'Allah engages the images of home and the diaspora in Ojaide's poetry and how they are presented with oral literary techniques, especially those bordering on Urhobo Udje. He also foregrounds Ojaide's use of animal symbolism to depict migration in the collection.

Mathias Orhero has explored the existentialist concepts of individualism and memory in the poetry of Ojaide and Robert Frost. He analyses Ojaide's *The Beauty I Have Seen* using the theory of existentialism and submits that "Ojaide is largely an existentialist in his outlook, especially in his recent collections of poetry, and his existentialist thought is engineered with experimental language and form" (135).

What can easily be gleaned from the brief review of literature presented above is that Ojaide's poetry has been engaged from various perspectives but apart from a few works that applied existentialist concepts in the analysis of Ojaide's poetry, the motif of disillusionment and absurdity in Ojaide's poetry, particularly his recent collections, is yet to receive sufficient attention.

The Theory of Existentialism

Existentialism is a philosophical theory that evolved in the early 20th century, and it examines the place of man in the universe. In an attempt to conceptualise existentialism, Aneela Malhotra submits that it is concerned with "the condition of the human existence, and individual emotions, actions, responsibilities, thoughts, and the existence of the human being in general. Existentialists focus more on the subjective rather than the objective aspects or knowledge in the human being such as the beliefs, religion, feelings, and emotions- freedom, pain, regret, guilt, anxiety, despair, finitude, alienation, and boredom" (6). Solomon Robert believes that existentialism is predicated upon the idea of an absurd world where everything is meaningless and void, and man has to find purpose and self-realisation in this seeming meaninglessness (1-2). Søren Kierkegaard is considered the father of the existentialist thought. Kierkegaard asserts that the individual is solely responsible for giving meaning to life and living life "authentically" (Kaufmann 37).

Existentialism evolved in the late 19th and early 20th centuries. Its development was a direct result of the socio-historical realities at the time. The first and second world wars caused the death of millions of people. Humans witnessed "unparalleled cruelties" and the rise of totalitarian ideologies (Sreekumar Nellickappilly 4). The pervading realities of loss, death, doubt, and suffering led to the dismounting of established views, notions, and philosophies.

The earliest existentialists questioned the fundamental nature of man, the universe, and the purpose of man in the universe. This, coupled with the feelings of despair caused by the world wars, made existentialists to question traditional ways of thinking. Monalisa Kalita examines the nature of existentialism vis-à-vis the background in which it evolved and concludes thus:

Existentialism may be characterized as a protest against all forms of rationalism. Secondly, it stands against mechanism and naturalism in the sphere of philosophical theory and in the sphere of social theory; it stands against all patterns of human organization and uniqueness of the individual person. Thirdly, it not only makes a drastic distinction between subjective and the objective truth but also gives priority to subjective truth. Fourthly, it regards man as fundamentally ambiguous and sees the human situation as filled with contradiction and tension which cannot be resolved by means of exact or consistent thinking. Lastly, stress upon freedom that can lead towards either faith in God or downright atheism. Thus, existentialism has produced both the most penetrating forms of Christian faith and the most nihilistic types of human self-assertion. (4)

There are specific themes which existentialism addresses. These themes have become central to existentialist thought and some of them are employed in this work. Apart from the major existentialist ethos of existence preceding essence, the specific existentialist concepts applied in this paper are disillusionment and absurdity.

Disillusionment is a central motif in existentialism. In existentialist philosophy, it is believed that the search for meaning, the realisation of meaninglessness in existence, and the confrontation with the absurd, birth disillusionment. The concept of disillusionment therefore recurs in existentialist literature. Disillusionment manifests in the form of depression, disappointment, pessimism and a general lack of hope. In existentialist thought, disillusionment is conceived, in one of Kierkegaard's early works entitled *Works of Love,* as follows:

When the God-forsaken worldliness of earthly life shuts itself in complacency, the confined air develops poison, the moment gets stuck and stands still, the prospect is lost, a need is felt for a refreshing, enlivening breeze to cleanse the air and dispel the poisonous vapors lest we suffocate in worldliness. ... Lovingly to hope all things is the opposite of despairingly to hope nothing at all. Love hopes all things—yet is never put to shame. To relate oneself expectantly to the possibility of the good is to hope. To relate oneself expectantly to the possibility of evil is to fear. By the decision to choose hope one decides infinitely more than it seems, because it is an eternal decision. (246-250)

Absurdity is also a dominant theme in existentialism. It derives from the concept of the absurd. The absurd, or Absurdism, owes its origins to the writings of Albert Camus, a renowned Algerian existentialist philosopher and writer. In his seminal masterpiece, *The Myth of Sisyphus*, Camus attempts to account for the futility of meaning and the search for meaning in existence. Camus posits that "in this unintelligible and limited universe, man's fate henceforth assumes its meaning. A horde of irrationals has sprung up and surrounds him until his ultimate end. In his recovered and now studied lucidity, the feeling of absurd becomes clear and definite" (21). To him, the absurd is a reality that humans cannot avoid; life itself is absurd. In relation to mainstream existentialist thought that foregrounds man's search for meaning, absurdists are of the belief that meaning is unattainable and man's existence is futile. Camus uses the Greek mythological character, Sisyphus, to demonstrate the absurdity of existence. Existentialists believe that the world is absurd and meaningless, and that man is cut off from any form of transcendentalism. Charlotte Keys writes that existentialists believe that humans "create gods, religions, and theologies because they want to believe the world is ordered and purposeful. According to the existentialists, responsibility for one's life lies entirely with oneself" (15). For them, man's consciousness is the only form of existence, and every other thing in the world is a creation of that existence. Absurdity manifests through pessimism, uncertainty, meaninglessness, hopelessness, and futility, among others.

Disillusionment in Tanure Ojaide's
Waiting for the Hatching of a Cockerel and *The Beauty I Have Seen*

In existentialist literature, disillusionment manifests as a theme, as well as through the agency of sub-themes like abandonment, disappointment, angst, dread, pain, depression, repression, pessimism, fear, and hopelessness, among others. All of these are evident in Ojaide's poetry in various forms.

Ojaide's "When a War Song Is a Love Song," reveals the motif of disillusionment. The poet's pessimism and disillusionment are revealed through the various vicissitudes of life faced by the characters that the poet creates. Harping on the pain of women, the poet persona reveals that: "Men sweat all right, but women weep; / their heads carry so much load as they / live with oppressors at home and outside" (*Waiting* 65). The said lines portray a bleak picture of women's plight, especially in the poet's African society. The despair of the poet at the ill-treatment of women is foregrounded as the poet persona says:

Every human deserves to carry smiles,

everybody deserves a breathing space;

every life deserves a share of happiness

....

It hurts to lie under a massive hulk

it hurts to be trampled upon;

it bleeds the heart to be caged

(*Waiting* 66).

    The above lines can be interpreted by the reader as the poet's revelation of despair and disillusionment at the way women are treated in a patriarchal society. The tone of pessimism and pain that is evident in the poem further underscores its themes of despair and disillusionment.

    Disillusionment is also revealed in the poet's depiction of a "grief-smothered mother" whose eldest son is deceased and a junior son "stares into vacant space / left by the dead, avoid the very room / once shared, and flees to another city" (*Waiting* 66). The reader can only imagine the pain and despair of the mother. This pain is a part of life that man is doomed to experience and accept. To further depict the despair of the "grief-smothered mother," the poet persona reveals the addiction of her husband as he "leaves home early and returns late, / drunk after wandering from door to door of hosts / who console him with bottles of the local brew"

    (*Waiting* 67). The woman's pain is compounded by the careless and reckless lifestyle of her supposed husband. Ojaide has used the sufferings of the woman in this poem to reveal despair and disillusionment as a part of life. The woman's husband avoids reality by taking to drunkenness, but she faces the reality heads on. She becomes the "existentialist hero" in the poem, the character that lives in despair and experiences disillusionment in existence yet accepts the reality.

    Ojaide's "Out of Step," employs the mode of satire and humour to reveal despair. The poet reveals his disappointment and frustration with the myopic behaviour of his people. In doing this, he satirises some of the shortcomings of his society and uses humour as a mode. The first few lines address the issue of superstition in his society, which the poet clearly frowns at:

They tell me witches have made the cherry fruit tree

their coven where they plot the death of their kinsfolk

who die of diabetes, stroke, heart-attack, and cancer.

These victims of witches did not guard against cholesterol

and had their fill of palm oil, coconut, and larded beef.

They relished their staple of starch, garri, yam, and rock salt

(*The Beauty* 108).

The poet's disappointment at the people's superstitious beliefs leads to the motif of disillusionment. The inability of the people to accept the truth for what it is, rather than ascribing their woes to other mythical sources, is a source of disappointment to the poet-persona. This is reflected in the second section of the poem where the poet-persona reveals the "goatish behaviour" of his people whose "heads" are "stuffed with starch in place of brains, / they walk on their heads where others sprint." There is the tone of hopelessness and pessimism in the said lines. The poet proceeds to show some absurd acts of his people and highlights his disappointment and disillusionment in the final line: "I have stopped reasoning with those who deny their own humanity" (109). The poet's satire of his society is realised through the tone of despair and disillusionment. To the reader, the poet persona is akin to Sisyphus, who accepts the reality of his existential despair and does not question the workings of the absurd in the world.

In Ojaide's "Today," the poet persona reflects upon his life and existence. In conveying the idea of meaninglessness in life, the persona reveals: "I am looking for a fruit in the wilds / that will purge me clean of daydream" (*The Beauty* 38). The reference to "daydream" represents life and its transience. To the persona, existence is short and surreal. The meaninglessness of existence is further echoed by the poet persona thus:

The day has laid siege to my hope;

my faith suffocates in a cell of lust.

Today the muse offers me manna

laced all over with shreds of misery

(*The Beauty* 38).

The above extract shows that the poet's existentialist vision of life is hopeless and full of misery. This vision is further expressed in the lines: "On earth paradise is a daydream; / dream must give way to wakeful life." Ojaide uses this epigram to comment on the harsh reality of life. It comments on the bleakness of life and relays the pessimism that existentialists are known for. To Ojaide, there is no "paradise" on earth. This invites the reader to reflect upon and accept the reality of the struggles that man must go through in life. Life is not a paradise where everything is perfect and everyone is happy. The reality of life is marked by pain, suffering, struggle, disillusionment, and futility. It is also ironic that the persona's "muse" offers him "manna" laced with "misery." This reveals the difficulty of human existence.

Ojaide's poetry expresses the twin themes of abandonment and alienation as forms of disillusionment. In "New Life," the poet persona invites the reader to "open arms to a lone soul." The "stranger" in the poem acts as an alienated man who has been abandoned by his society. His alienation is not just psychological but also physical. He is dislocated and homeless. To show that to the reader, the poet persona says:

Take in the stranger at the doorstep

don't for fear of robbers let him die;

give him a bowl to drink from,

share what the family can afford;

he could be the god you have

been praying to for safe travel;

he could be the one out there

sent to help you out of a trap

(*Waiting* 145).

In the above lines, the poet harps on the plight of the alienated such as the stranger and calls for the need to embrace him. Alienation and abandonment are presented as unsavoury plights in order for the reader's emotion to be stirred. Furthermore, the poet, through the persona of Aminogbe, philosophises on man's ultimate alienation by employing the metaphor of "travel" to represent man's transit through existence. In this transit, the poet persona avers, "you will one day step out and not know / who waits for you at the journey's end; / no sense of the face in your front" (145). The poet's idea of solitary existence is conveyed through the tone of uncertainty prevalent in the lines. The poet also shows the theme of alienation and abandonment through the "Ojojo schoolgirl," who is "nameless" and whom "nobody knows" (147). The schoolgirl is abandoned by the society and cast into physical and psychological alienation. This happens before she "forfeits her delight / to feed a hungry one." By juxtaposing her plight and that of "another beggar stung with indifference," the poet is able to show the inherent truth of existence that one is individually abandoned to his/her own fate and left to make meaning of life and existence by himself/herself.

Ojaide's "Without a Guide" thematises the abandonment and alienation of the poet persona by his muse. The poem begins by introducing the theme thus: "After the crossroads the minstrel looks back- / his guide has performed a disappearing act" (*The Beauty* 19). The "disappearing act" of the guide refers to the absence of transcendental beings in human existence. Fate and faith have no place in existentialist thought and the idea of man's abandonment and consequent alienation serves to convey this. Having been abandoned by his "guide," the poet persona "must take the rest of the long road alone." The metaphor of "long road" describes human existence, with its long-winding path. Man must go through existence with the knowledge that he is alone with his thoughts. The realities of existence are revealed as the poet persona evolves from the level of phantasmagorical reality. He realises that there are:

no invisible hands taking over toilsome tasks.

No more will the gates open to herald his arrival,

nor the cherry tree wait for him to shower fruits.

He must personally roast or boil the yam he grows to eat;

No "Food is ready!" or a laid-out table to select his fill (19)

The above extract shows the poe- persona's acknowledgment of his alienation and abandonment. The lines reveal the idea of disillusionment as obvious in the poet's reflective tone.

Absurdity in Tanure Ojaide's
Waiting for the Hatching of a Cockerel and *The Beauty I Have Seen*

The motif of absurdity manifests in the poetry of Ojaide through his treatment of socio-political or ecological affairs. Ojaide's *Waiting* employs absurdity in the presentation of various issues. In "The Fate of our Lingua Franca," Ojaide employs the theme of absurdity to reflect his ecological vision. Using the persona of Aminogbe, the poem thematises the gradual loss of the poet's natural environment due to the activities of oil companies. The poem opens with the poet- persona's recollection of "childhood delights" such as "wild apples, cherries, grapes, and breadfruit / garnered from the forest, his provider" (69). The environment was pristine, and the forests "remained evergreen from rain." The poem further says that:

Creeks and rivers flowed all year round

and fishing with hooks brought home

fresh and salt water fish – catfish and

mudfish ...

The poet persona's conception of the universe was essentially "green." Their reality becomes absurd when the oil companies exploit the natural resources belonging to the people. The poet shows the pain and sufferings of the people, using the images of "outbreaks of seizures and rashes" and "fire from above," which the "folks have to bear till they drop / into hell, a shell of their proud selves" (70). The reader can see the plight of the people as a mirror of the human condition – hopeless, brutish, and painful. The depiction of the horrors caused by the activities of the oil companies is employed as a metaphor of human absurdity, depicted as the insensitivity of one to the wellbeing of another.

Aminogbe becomes the symbol of "man" in the poem, and his search for meaning in the absurdity created by the "oil companies" can be interpreted as man's search for meaning in an absurd world.

Absurdity presents itself in "Fatalities" through the depiction of a bleak vision of life. The poet philosophizes on the nature of existence and the absurd. Through the use of metaphors and symbols, he shows that life is hopeless and the struggle for meaning in existence is futile. The poem starts with the lines: "Planted in the soil, these heads / won't grow –unlike pieces of yam" (*Waiting* 98). The yam heads are used as symbols for life's absurdity, staleness, hopelessness, and frustration. As typical in the existentialist tradition, the poet persona does not blame "the overbearing sun," "faint stars," and the "voracious earth" but accepts the reality of absurdity. Existentialists believe that man alone is responsible for his fortunes and misfortunes, and, thus, blames cannot be apportioned to anyone or anything, transcendental or physical. The absurdity of life is further shown through the poet's reference to a "cemetery," the symbol of death and the ultimate end of man in absurdist thought. In the poem, the "cemetery devours adjoining streets / and the living have only a short time / to wait for their inevitable turn" (98). The preceding lines echo the absurdity of life in clear terms. Man's existence is short and the only certain thing is that he will be devoured by the "cemetery." Man can only wait for his "inevitable turn." The poet's bleak vision of life is also reflected in the next stanza:

The time has passed when in wakes

people laughed, drank, and danced

their relatives fell from over-ripeness

or from ill winds that barriers

of herbs and barks couldn't break-

the living woke from dreams

of becoming future ancestors (98)

The permeating mood in the excerpt above is that of sadness and death, both shades of absurdity. In the poem, the only certainty of humans is "becoming future ancestors." Images and symbols of death saturate the poem and they include "skeletons in dust," "grave shadow," and "ghostly hands." The poet's depictions of death, pessimism, hopelessness, pain, and loss are all representations of life's ultimate meaninglessness. Proving that life is absurd to everyone, the poet presents a "twelve-year old" who says "I have neither father nor mother / to bring home food; also all my / uncles, aunts, and cousins gone" (99). The universe seems unfair, and man's existence seems useless. That is the vision of the absurd.

The reader can identify the theme of absurdity in Ojaide's *The Beauty*. Using the persona of a wandering minstrel, Ojaide engages this theme with the subtexts of socio-political or ecological activism. In "Today," the poet persona reveals the absurdity of existence to the reader. The poem starts thus: "Today the muse trashes my craft, / and that's not all I suffer in one day" (38). Having established the idea of suffering, which is associated with absurdity, the poet persona goes further to evoke feelings of absurdity and the meaninglessness of life:

> I am looking for a fruit in the wilds
>
> that will purge me clean of daydream.
>
> The day has laid siege to my hope;
>
> my faith suffocates in a cell of lust.
>
> Today the muse offers me manna
>
> laced all over with shreds of misery. (38)

The reader can observe the pessimism of the poet's tone as he employs his "muse" as a metaphor for life. Even "faith," hope that is, serves no purpose as everything is laced with "misery." This is why he goes further to assert that "On earth paradise is a daydream; / dream must give way to wakeful life." The lines show the poet's bleak vision of life. He believes that "paradise" or a happy ending is a myth that man must do away with. This vision is comparable to that of Albert Camus in *The Myth of Sisyphus* where Sisyphus' eternal punishment mirrors the entire human condition. To the poet, life is a "paradise of pain" filled with a "plethora of stabs" (*The Beauty* 39). These images are pessimistic and absurdist. The reader is conducted through the incongruity of life and the existentialist vision of this poem.

Ojaide's "Waiting" thematises absurdity and shares the motif of waiting as in Samuel Beckett's *Waiting for Godot*. Beckett's play is canonical in existentialist drama for its peculiar absurdist vision and conveyance of existential meaninglessness. In Camus' *The Myth of Sisyphus*, the Sisyphean myth is alluded to. In the myth, Sisyphus pushes a boulder up a hill only for the boulder to roll back down for Sisyphus to do so again for all eternity (John Finley 593). Coated with satire, Ojaide's "Waiting" presents absurdity through the existentialist idea of eternity. The ideas of eternal recurrence and patience, as well as of waiting, are presented in the absurdist form to the reader. The poem is short and this shortness symbolises the transient nature of existence. The poet echoes the absurdity of eternal and futile waiting thus:

>The elders advise us to wait till we grow old;
>
>wow, we wait for their privileges till we are told.
>
>The politicians tell us to wait till their second term;
>
>hurray, wait for prosperity till after we re-elect them.
>
>The dreamers teach us to watch till they wake;
>
>yes, wait till they make it to another daybreak.
>
>They always ask us to keep on waiting all the time;
>
>yes, learn from them to wait out an entire lifetime (50).

In the preceding lines, the reader identifies the absurdity in "waiting," which is a major motif in the poem. The poet persona laments the endless waiting for "elders," "politicians," and "dreamers." These characters are used to echo various shades of humanity, namely: elders, the sustaining factor in humanity whose duty is to guide, to advise, and to lead the way; politicians, who are responsible for the control and distribution of resources for the welfare of humanity; dreamers, the visioners/prophets who represent the religious base of humanity. When these factors, as they are here demonstrated, fail in their responsibilities, humanity is thrown into the abyss of meaninglessness.

Parallelism and repetition are employed in the poem. They are used to convey the Sisyphean idea of eternal recurrence and the absurdity in waiting for too many things when none has been achieved. The poet throws political satire into this existentialist mix when he creates the image of "politicians" telling "us to wait till their second term / ... for prosperity" (50). By alluding to this crop of politicians, the poet merges existentialist vision with socio-political activism. The pessimistic tone of the poem reaches its peak when the poet reveals that "they always ask us / ... to wait out an entire lifetime" (50). Waiting forever for someone or something that does not appear to be forthcoming echoes the Beckettian idea of waiting endlessly for the unknown.

Ojaide presents absurdity in his poetry through the use of rhetorical questions. "Suspending the End," in Ojaide's *Waiting*, poses a number of rhetorical questions that invites the reader to ponder over existence and the problems that beleaguer humanity. The poem opens with the first question: "On the road ahead, / how many crossroads / with forks to dead ends?" (155). This rhetorical question echoes the uncertainty and meaninglessness of life. A reader can interpret "crossroads" as the various paths that life can take while "dead ends" can be seen as the ultimate purposelessness of life. This question, therefore, invites the reader to ponder upon life's ultimate absurdity.

Another rhetorical question in the poem is "will bends deflect vision / or break resolve to arrive?" (155). This question foregrounds the wavering nature of life as seen in the poet's use of "bends." The poet attempts to show how the uncertainty of life will cause a period of existential crises where man has to choose to continue to find meaning in existence or give it up as a lost cause. The final question extracted from this poem is: "Will we cover the distance / without trading off the future?" (156). This question presents the issue of choice to the reader. It is a question of whether or not man can live life without making decisions and choices that will affect the future. Since existentialists place a premium on choice and freewill, as well as uncertainty of the future, it is plausible that the poet persona poses this question to reflect on the imperfection of human choice because no matter the choice man makes, he is certain to confront life's ultimate absurdity.

Ojaide also employs symbolism in the thematisation of absurdity. Ojaide uses the river as a symbol in "The Minstrel Comes to a River" in *The Beauty*. The poem thematises the vicissitudes of life that man must go through in the search for meaning. Through the persona of a wandering minstrel, Ojaide uses the river as a symbol of the absurd. In the opening line, the poet-persona "staggers into a deep river" (21). The river is described as a "swirling water snake whose shocks / make a simple mishap in the crossing a mortal crisis" (21). The description of the river further reveals its symbolism of life's absurd realities. The nature of the absurd in existence is captured in the lines: "if he puts behind this river that already leers at him, / he still has six more to cross to claim victory over rivals" (21). The "six more" rivers to cross represent the multitudinous nature of existential adversity that man must face. The poem ends with the lines:

> A river does not end the minstrel's journey;
> it halts him to muse on land and water
> until he realises that all he has is only his song.
> The minstrel meets a river, dreads nightfall. (22)

The submission that a river does not "end the minstrel's journey" reflects stoicism and the realisation of the absurd as the nature of existence. The river, therefore, symbolises not only the absurd but also the transcendency of material/physical existence, as well as the existential stoicism that comes with the realisation of the place of the absurd in man's life. This realisation is revealed through the permanence of "song," capable of transiting existence. The poet persona has only his "song" even with the reality that the "river" does not end. "Nightfall" symbolises death. This is the ultimate meaninglessness of life and of existence; everything amounts to nothing. The minstrel's journey across the river ultimately ends in nightfall. To the reader, this can be interpreted as the futility and despair that comes with the lifelong search and struggle for meaning in the universe.

Conclusion

This paper has examined the motifs of disillusionment and absurdity in Ojaide's *Waiting for the Hatching of a Cockerel* and *The Beauty I Have Seen*. It reveals that Ojaide has employed the existentialist concepts of disillusionment and absurdity in the presentation of his personal vision as well as his socio-political, cultural, and ecological activism. Some of the stylistic strategies with which Ojaide presents his existentialist ideas are also discussed in this paper. Drawing from the analysis in this work, it can be stated that Ojaide's poetry expresses the philosophy of existentialism. It is also obvious that his recent collections show existentialist reflections on the human condition. The recommendation here is that further studies should be carried out on the newer poetry collections so that the vision, aesthetics, and artistic directions of the poems and the poet can be established through different perspectives.

Works Cited

Aiyejina, Funso. "Recent Nigerian Poetry in English: An Alter-Native Tradition." *Komparatistische Hefte* 15.16 (1987): 49-64.

Alu, Nesther, and Vashti Suwa. "Tanure Ojaide: The Poet-Priest of the Niger-Delta and the Land Saga." *AFRREV LALIGENS: An International Journal of Language, Literature and Gender Studies* 1.1 (2012): 132-144.

Baird, Forrest, and Walter Kaufmann. *From Plato to Derrida*. Pearson Prentice Hall, 2008.

Balogun, Jide. "The Poet as a Social Crusader: Tanure Ojaide and the Poetry of Intervention." *Journal of Humanities* 20 (2006): 78-88.

Bassey, Ude Bassey. "Forms of Political Consciousness in the Poetry of Tanure Ojaide: A Study of the *Endless Song* and *When It No Longer Matters Where You Live*." *African Research Review* 5.2 (2011): 168-176.

Camus, Albert. *The Myth of Sisyphus, and Other Essays*. Vintage Books, 1955.

Copleston, Frederick. "Existentialism." *Philosophy* 23.84 (2009): 19–37.

Kalita, Monalisa. *Existentialism of Kierkegaard: A Critical Study*. Thesis. Gauhati University, 2015.

Keys, Charlotte. *Shakespeare's Existentialism*. Thesis. University of London, 2012.

Kierkegaard, Søren. *Works of Love*. Harper Collins, 1962.

Malhotra, Aneela. *A Comparative Study of the Aspects of Existentialism in the Novels of Anita Desai and Arun Joshi*. Thesis. Bharati Vidyapeeth Deemed University, 2015.

Nellickappilly, Sreekumar. "Aspects of Western Philosophy." *NPTEL Online Courses*.

Ojaide, Tanure. *Waiting for the Hatching of a Cockerel*. Africa World Press, 2008.

—-. *The Beauty I Have Seen: A Trilogy*. Malthouse Press, 2010.

Ojaruega, Enajite Eseoghene. "The Place of Urhobo Folklore in Tanure Ojaide's Poetry." *Tydskrif vir Letterkunde* 52.2 (2015): 138-158.

Okediji, Moyo. "Maggots of Naija's Rotten Flesh". *The Protest Art Studio*.

Okome, Onookome. "Introduction: Tanure Ojaide: The Poet Laureate of the Niger Delta." *Writing the Homeland: The Poetry and Politics of Tanure Ojaide.* African Studies Series, 2002. 9-18.

Orhero, Mathias Iroro. "Individualism and Memory: Robert Frost and Tanure Ojaide." *Tydskrif vir letterkunde* 54.2 (2017): 122-135.

Robert, Solomon. *Existentialism*. McGraw-Hill, 1974.

Kaufmann, Walter. *Existentialism: From Dostoevsky to Sartre*. World Publishing, 1956.

The Signification of Spirituality in Selected Short Stories of Tanure Ojaide

Enajite Eseoghene Ojaruega

Introduction

Modern African literature generally reflects the realities of the African condition and existence. That reality includes the norms, values, superstitions, philosophies, traditions and other belief systems peculiar to the African by virtue of lived experiences. For African writers, art is a mirror of reality; hence one can say that African literature incorporates and interrogates the historical and cultural worldview of the people. Since literature is a cultural production, African writers consciously or unconsciously, in their literary representations, often reflect the lived experiences of their people. This is why some beliefs and practices which are specific to some groups or make meaning to them form the backdrop of a writer's work. Hence, cultural theory expects the signification of material and non-material things such as belief systems as well as how they are represented physically through nature. These factors are important in discussing the works of a writer grounded in the culture, myths, legends, and belief systems of his or her people.

According to Tanure Ojaide, people who share the same birthplace, culture, and society are connected in their group values and interests (236). This assertion is underscored in literary studies by Abiloa Irele's observation that the concern with historical and sociological realities makes African literature a more accurate and comprehensible account of contemporary African reality than sociological or political documents. It is for this reason that I intend to use African culture in general and Urhobo/Pan-Edo culture in particular to study the signification of spirituality in selected short stories of Ojaide. Culture is used here in its broadest implication.

Much as Tanure Ojaide is best known as a poet, he is also a fiction writer and has through the decades published novels and collections of short stories. His short stories collections include: *God's Medicine-Men and Other Stories* (2004), *The Debt-Collector and Other Stories* (2009) and *The Old Man in a State House and Other Stories (2012)*. His stories are marked by cultural reflection that sets his characters, narration, and thematic preoccupations apart from other short writers such as Chinua Achebe from the Igbo-speaking part of Nigeria and Ngugi wa Thiong'o from the Gikuyu area of Kenya. Ojaide's nativity is inextricably connected to his vision and perspective as a writer. He has himself admitted that the writer is not an "air-plant" but one rooted in a specific place which has its geography and culture.

Many scholars, including this writer, have written extensively on the influence of Urhobo orature in Ojaide's poetry. His novels, especially *The Activist*, have also received critical exegeses in the areas of environmental activism and female agency. Generally, Ojaide's works are suffused with substance and symbolisms that underscore his unapologetic identification with his Urhobo cultural heritage. However, not much scholarly attention has been accorded his three collections. His interest in the invisible and intangible forces at play in the lives of characters in his short stories has not been explored. Similarly, quite a number of critical scholarships have been done on his writings and the folkloric elements in them, but I will use some of his short stories to interrogate the nature and importance of spirituality which appear to reflect aspects of his people's worldviews. The writer projects this mainly through their beliefs in, for example, the relationship between the living and the dead, the importance of the final resting place for the dead, the existence and operations of supernatural forces capable of oppressive and sexual attacks, as well as the efficacy of bewitchment on the living. Ojaide's interest in these subjects are consistently expressed and reflected in the characters, setting, and thematic concerns in his short stories, yet it has not received commensurate critical attention.

Conceptualising Spirituality in African Literature and Society

As a renowned African scholar of religion and philosophy, Mbiti believes the African life is filled with spirituality. An important aspect of the African belief system has to do with the concept of the existence of two parallel worlds. Commenting on this, Soyinka argues that the African reality can be best understood as a simultaneous inhabitation of the world of the living and the dead as well as the present and the past. He says further that it is the tension between all these coordinates that forms the primary object of mimesis for African art and by extension its literature. In trying to explain this connection in the Urhobo culture, Tonukari writes:

Traditional Urhobo basically views the universe as comprising of two realms: the universe and the invisible. Humans occupy the former while divinities, ancestors, myriads of unnamed spirits/forces dwell in the latter. While less powerful, the human world is the center of attention. Ancestors are essentially benevolent spirits –they know and have their families' interest at heart. (npag.)

To the African, spirituality involves beliefs and practices that relate to human life. Sickness, for example, is not only a state of being physically unhealthy but could also connote an imbalance in one's psychological and spiritual life. Although many Africans today have abandoned their various forms of traditional worship or veneration, and embraced non-indigenous religions, the average African is still highly spiritual and still believes in the existence and influence of forces beyond the ordinary in human life. These forces could be benevolent or malevolent. They could be responsible for turns in one's fortune for better or for worse. In cases where benevolent forces at work, humans experience a state of well-being in life's endeavors, while, malevolent forces cause sickness or bad fortune and so require a search for solution or methods of amelioration through supernatural interventions.

Ojaide's stories set in his Agbon and other places reflect the life lived around him. Agbon is a clan in Urhobo land comprising of seven sub-clans into which the writer was born. What happens in real life also happens in fiction. It is only that fiction sometimes imagines and stretches the humanly possible into fantasy. That is why many aspects of the spiritual fall into the realm of fantasy and myth. The realism that the fiction writer thus aims at is to express the humanly possible even in the imaginary. As far as the invisible and spiritual are concerned in these stories, they are the indigenous beliefs and myths that permeate the characters and ideas of many Africans, including many educated Christianized and Islamized among them.

In Ojaide's short stories, he pries into the characters and, often using the omnipresent narrator's viewpoint, shines a searchlight into the complexities of life as lived in the respective environments representing the settings in the stories, hence some of his short stories treat the theme of the relationship between the living and the dead. What comes out of these stories is that there are alternative realities in the physical mundane life and the spiritual life. The visible and invisible, which though are contrastive, are expected to merge into one to define a human existence. In other words, the physical and visible must be in agreement with the invisible and spiritual for human life to have harmony and peace.

Elsewhere, Ojaide has written of the "Urhoro" of the Urhobo people which indicates a pre-human existence, which some describe as life in the womb, where people choose their respective destinies before being born to live them out. This again shows that in his understanding of the Urhobo culture, the spiritual precedes the physical which it collaborates with in life before going back to a spiritual state upon death. In this conception, life is cyclical, moving from the spiritual to the physical and back to the spiritual in an unending cycle. This spiritual or rather supernatural state affects the Urhobo and other Africans who believe in them and many people spend their time and resources to protect themselves from malefactors in the forms of witches, wizards, and other evil forces.

In Ojaide's short stories, therefore, the reader encounters two worlds—the visible and the invisible, both real in man's physical and emotional/psychological life. The binaries of myth and reality are collapsed into the traditional belief system under which many of the fictional characters in the writer's stories operate. Though one is visible and the other invisible, there is no boundary between the spiritual and physical in the lives of the characters. This could also be described in the sense of reality and fantasy, a blend of which is an important aspect of the spirituality exercised by the characters. These two aspects of life, though one is visible and the other invisible, are realities or put in another way "alternative realities" of life.

The Signification of Spirituality in Selected Short Stories of Tanure Ojaide

"The Benevolence of the Dead" from *The Old Man in a State House* is one of the short stories Ojaide uses to represent the visible and the invisible, the living and the dead, and their connectedness. The narrator is a young girl who loses her father at an early age and has to live with an uncle who mistreats her. He starves her, engages her in arduous tasks, and refuses to cater for her educational needs. One particular night, after having prayed fervently to God for succor from her sufferings, her father visits her in her sleep. Apparently, he is able to see her pitiable plight from his abode of the dead in the invisible world. The little girl's earnest plea for help brings the dead father back to the land of the living as a spirit being. He interacts with her, counsels her not to worry and assures her that all will be well for her. Things turn out well for her as her dead father has assured her in her sleep. He is a benevolent spirit and a guardian who somehow manages from his spirit-world to give her emotional and psychological support as well as ensure that others still alive give his daughter the material and financial support that she needs to develop herself as a young girl.

The foregoing is in consonance with an Urhobo belief that the death of a relative does not end the affinity between the living and the dead. Ottuh explains:

The dead pass through the gates to the spiritual realm when all necessary rituals have been performed. As the departed are never regarded as being really dead in the grave, their offspring and other relations still refer to them as their fathers, mothers, brothers or sisters, which they were before their transition.

They are believed to be capable of exercising their parental roles or so, though now in a more powerful and unrestricted way, over their survivors (212).

Tanure Ojaide portrays a mystical relationship between the living and the dead in the aforementioned story. It is only the narrator who sees and interacts freely with her father whenever he appears to her. It is significant that the man wears the same clothes he was used to wearing when he was alive. However, the writer describes his eyes as if they were stars. So, in appearing to his daughter, the dead father carries both human and non-human qualities. After their encounter in the girl's sleep, the dead father leaves walking backwards. The Urhobo generally attribute to ghosts such weird behavior such as walking backwards (the living are not supposed to do).

In any case, on his part, the late father keeps a close watch over his daughter and is sensitive to her travails. He always appears to encourage and reassure her at crucial moments when she is facing some difficulties. This intervention gives her the stability she requires to thrive as a young woman. For her father, he is at peace in the spirit realm knowing that he is able to perform his parental responsibilities towards her even though he is not physically with her. All he asks of her is to "Always remain a good girl!" (6). However, towards the end of the story, he seems to abandon her after she sleeps with her boyfriend when she had not graduated from school. One possible interpretation for this is that as a spirit being, his duty has been to guide and guard her through a period when she was relatively innocent, vulnerable, and helpless. That she now has another male companion, a lover, could mean he feels his assignment regarding her welfare has been completed and he can quietly retire back to his abode in the invisible world. The young woman will henceforth learn how to cope with life's challenges from her own experience. Ojaide implies also that there are physical consequences for disobeying the injunctions or expectations of the dead or spiritual forces. In "The Benevolence of the Dead", we can infer that the spirit of the late father distances itself from the daughter the moment she has sexual intercourse with her boyfriend. His only expectation from her as he helps her navigate through life's difficulties is that she should "always remains a good girl" which she promises to. However, when she violates this pact, he separates himself from her physically and spiritually. In the course of this narrative, Ojaide's also reveals the mutually beneficial relationship which exists between the living and the dead. In the above story, the father is roused from his resting place in the spirit world to come to his daughter's aid in her moments of great need in the human world. He is at peace knowing he is able to ameliorate his daughter's sufferings while the daughter, on her part, experiences a measure of progress and emotional balance from her father's spiritual presence in her life.

This concept of filial responsibility and obligation, between the living and the dead, is depicted via a reverse perspective in "The Debt-Collector," the title story of Ojaide's second short story collection where it becomes the duty of the relatives to redeem the image and ensure the well-being of the dead. In this story, the corpse of Ituru, a debtor who has been unable to pay back the money he owes his creditor, Shegbe, is forcibly seized by the rich man. This throws the family of the bereaved into double grief for a number of reasons that are culture-related. First, this act amounts to a violation of the spirit of the dead man as the Urhobo, and by extension African, concept of death recognizes the need to accord the body of the dead a final resting place within his family stead into which he returns in his next life. If Ituru's corpse is not reclaimed from his creditor, then "their family would be depleted by one adult: dead or alive" (26) and his "spirit will continue to haunt us" (28). In his article, Agbegbedia describes this relationship in the context of Urhobo culture thus:

…the Urhobo worldview embraces the belief that what we referred to as extended family (*orua*) in this mundane community of people has been pre-existent in the spiritual world (*erivwin*). For them therefore, beings are released from there to populate this earth and at death, one returns to it….Therefore among the Urhobo, there is a belief in what is called *erivwinr'uwevwin* (the spiritual abode of the household), *erivwinr'orua* (spiritual abode of the extended family)….This explains among other purposes, patri-linear family system inclusive, why the Urhobo like Biblical ancient Israelites bury their dead ones in the homestead of their fathers to make sure that when he or she would re-incarnate he or she would come back to life through the same family (59).

Yet another reason why the family of the deceased is anxious is that the family's honor is at stake. They can become the butt of cruel jokes, negative references and social stigmatization for generations to come because of Ituru's "shame of indebtedness" (27). A third factor is the fear that the captor might tamper with some vital body parts of the dead for ritual purposes and if the dead reincarnates, these body parts will ostensibly be missing. The family thus resolves that "We cannot shelve our responsibilities. He was ours and still ours. Let us save our man from disgrace – he cannot be a worthy ancestor buried in the bush belonging to the chief" (28). By the evening of the same day, the family lives up to this collective charge and raise the remaining forty pounds which their dead member owed. They return the money to Shegbe who also releases the corpse to them for the final burial. The timely intervention by the living members of Ituru's family affords the dead man respect and a peaceful place of rest in the realm of the spirits and among the pantheon of ancestors.

The above examples depict the mutually beneficial relationship that exists between characters in the visible and invisible worlds as portrayed in some of Ojaide's short stories. The dead is seen going out of its way to come back to life to guide and guard the interests and good fortunes of the living as in "The Benevolence of the Dead", while the living do not shirk their duty of restoring the honor of the dead and ensuring their smooth transition or passage to the world of the spirits as in "The Debt-Collector."

The theme of separation as a result of disobeying the spiritual is found in "Sharing Love" in Ojaide's *The Old Man in a State House and Other Short Stories*. The narrator and beautiful Kena are very much in love but are eventually forced to part ways because Kena is a "Mami Wata pickin" (62) and already married to a spirit husband who inhabits the marine world but comes at night to possess her. Despite several warnings from Kena's parents that they are not allowed to be together because Kena is already committed to a spirit spouse, both lovers decide to elope to the United States of America. After Kena and her boyfriend enjoy three days without any problem, Kena falls sick and no medical tests in different hospitals is able to diagnose the cause of the headache she is experiencing. Unable to find a medical solution to her condition abroad, Kena returns home to look for a cure. On returning to Nigeria, she resumes her relationship with the spirit lover who heals her because she spiritually belongs to 'him.'

Ojaide underscores the idea that the forces that inhabit and operate from the spirit realm are very powerful and disobeying them or going against their wishes will only cause more problems for the living especially those with whom they share a relationship. Kena is a person of two worlds as she appears comfortable with each partner in both disparate love relationships. She has a consensual relationship with her spirit husband who does not mind sharing her love with the human lover in so far as all the parties respect and maintain a tacit understanding. The spirit lover "owns" her at night but the boyfriend can have her during the day. The spiritual husband only demonstrates his hold over her when Kena and her boyfriend try to outsmart him by relocating out of the country. Eloping to the United States from Nigeria does not stop Kena's spiritual experience. By implication, the African belief is that nobody can hide from spiritual forces that affect them by leaving one place to a distant one.

While it is possible to have mutually satisfying contacts between human and spirit beings, Ojaide also presents a non-consensual association in "God's Medicine-Men," the title story of *God's Medicine-Men and Other Stories*. Endurance, the protagonist of the story, contends with some strange experiences. In school, she is often attacked by an invisible and oppressive weight called an incubus or succubus. She goes home to look for a solution to this problem and is confronted with another dilemma: she gets sexually violated by an invisible presence. In spite of her efforts she could "…not stop the intruder from entering into her at will. She wore rousers to bed, and yet she woke with a feeling of sticky wetness between her legs" (69). Worse still is that she is the daughter of a pastor and has been brought up in the Christian way to believe that evil forces have no power over her. Yet her prayers do not have any effect on the source or subject responsible for these forceful invasions. This creates anxiety in her and causes her physical and emotional stress. Her friend introduces her to Pastor Odele who combines his Christian worship with that of Olokun, the traditional river goddess. He recommends a spiritual bath in Sakpoba River to rid her of these oppressive forces at work in her life after which she gets some reprieve.

The manner through which Endurance's predicament is finally resolved calls to question the practice of some modern day clergymen. Clearly, some of them seek and employ powers beyond the scope of their Christian faith. Pastor Odele may claim to be a man of the Christian God by virtue of carrying a small Bible, but he has no church to take his followers. He seems to be a charlatan and combines Christianity with traditional religion (the worship of the water goddess known as Olokun or Mami Wata); hence he and others like Pastor Efe (whom he later 'empowers') are referred to as "God's medicine-men." Ironically too, the writer seems to suggest that there are some spiritual problems which require similar solutions, unorthodox as they may be, but which are capable of restoring balance and harmony to troubled individuals.

Ojaide engages the manifestation of spirituality in his short fiction by examining the effects of superstitious beliefs on the psyche and lifestyle of a person or community. In both "The Cherry Tree Palaver" and "Nobody Loves Me," Ojaide presents characters whose minds are conditioned to ascribe their problems to the manipulations of spiritual forces. Once this situation arises, such people are bound to act on this impulse as troubled and seek spiritual healing. This may be despite the fact that these people are only imagining negative forces are against them. Among the Urhobo and other Africans, many people attribute their sicknesses and poverty to spiritual attacks. This leads many to worry and seek salvation or healing from any source available to them; hence many go to traditional healers or to Pentecostal pastors for assistance.

In "The Cherry Tree Palaver," the people of Unoh village have become disenchanted with the ageless cherry tree and seek "the destruction of the tree's resident demon" (38) by cutting it down. The people experience short lifespan because of their unhealthy habits but put the blame on witches and evil spirits that meet in coven on that tree. Clearly, the poor villagers lack scientific knowledge to relate their unhealthy lifestyles to people dying young. Worse still, the exuberant pastor and his member exploit their naivety. Their superstition makes them believe that the sap of the old tree as they cut it down is the blood of the victims of witchcraft. It is significant that, in that story, an educated son who is a scientist, a professor of Botany, and skeptical from the outset about the people's views, and his superstitious father converge in views at the end of the story. The cutting down of the old tree has not stopped people from dying young. The sturdy cherry tree becomes a signification of ignorance that leads to superstitions. Ojaide seems to be saying in that story that many of the conditions attributed to spiritual attacks in Urhobo society (and other parts of Africa) are most likely as a result of ignorance that leads to senseless action as the cutting down of the ageless tree and the destruction of the eco-system of the area.

Ngozi, in "Nobody Loves Me," is a very beautiful woman at the prime of her womanhood. However, she is unable to attract the attention of men to seek for her love or fall in love with her despite her frantic efforts. She is troubled by all manners of thoughts and even remembers:

…that her elder sister was still living a spinster at forty-five in Aba. Is it true that the female children of her mother were jinxed not to have men? An old aunt had died after confessing that nothing could be done to remove the curse she had placed on her mother's children (107).

She seeks the assistance of a medicine man but her situation does not change for the better. She falls into depression and she ends up committing suicide because she feels nobody loves her. Depression in many traditional African societies is often associated with being bewitched. Many people suffering from severe depression, as in bi-polar cases, tend to "hear voices" and traditional healers tend to be consulted to stop such patients from hearing such voices. Ngozi's case did not degenerate to that extent before she takes her own life. It appears that she has low self-esteem and that may have been responsible for her not having male admirers even in a predominantly HIV/AIDS community. Her problems appear to be psychological and may not have the spiritual dimension she relates it to.

Conclusion

From the stories discussed, Tanure Ojaide presents characters whose outer and inner lives are associated with spiritual dimensions. Even though there are visible and invisible aspects to the lives of the characters, their portrayal is realistic in the sense that these aspects are interwoven in reality. Some aspects of the invisible and spiritual may look like fantasy (such as the dead counseling the living, a lover or husband in the spirit world having a wife in the living world, and witches meeting at night in coven on top of a cherry tree) but these are beliefs that humans harbor in their minds. The physical and the spiritual have to be in tandem with each other for emotional and psychological peace and harmony. They have to be reconciled in the destinies of humans to survive the actions of evil humans and spirits. Ojaide's characters live the spiritual world in the physical world. Both world coalesce to determine the reality of the living.

Works Cited

Agbegbedia, Anthony Oghenevwoke. "An Evaluation of the Urhobo Cultural Conception of Death." *Ogirisi: A New Journal of African Studies*. Vol. 11, 2015. 44-64.

Irele, Abiola. *The African Experience in Literature and Ideology*. Heinemann, 1981.

Mbiti, John Samuel. *African Religion and Philosophy.* Heinemann, 1990.

Ojaide, Tanure. *God's Medicine-Men and Other Stories*. Malthouse Press Limited, 2012.

—————————-. *The Old Man in a State House and Other Stories*. African Heritage Press, 2012.

—————————-. *The Debt- Collector and Other Stories*. Africa World Press, 2009.

—————————-. "The Niger Delta, Nativity and My Writing." *African Cultural and Economic Landscapes*. Edited by Paul Tiyambe Zeleza and Ezekiel Kalipeni. Africa World Press, 1999. 233-248.

Ojaruega, Enajite Eseoghene. "The Place of Urhobo Folklore in Tanure Ojaide's Poetry." *Tydskrif Vir Letterkunde*. 52 (2), 2015. 138-158.

Otite, Onigu. *The Urhobo People*. Heinemann, 1983.

Ottuh, John Arierhi. "The Urhobo Traditional Theologumenon on Afterlife and ChristianTheology of Eschatology: A Comparative Study." *Africology: The Journal of Pan African Studies*. Vol. 10, No 3, May 2017. 203-220.

Soyinka, Wole. *Myth, Literature and the African World.* .Cambridge University Press, 1976.

Tonukari, Ochuko. "Urhobo Community as Unity of Two Worlds." Urhobo Historical-Society.Web.
http://www.waado.org/UrhoboCulture/Religion/tonukari/Urhobo_commun

Poetics of Dissidence:

Nigeria's Political Landscape in Tanure Ojaide's *The Activist* and *Matters of the Moment*

Zaynab Ango

Introduction

In *The Activist* and *Matters of the Moment,* Tanure Ojaide engages Nigeria's post-independence political landscape. *The Activist* depicts the phenomenon of oil production in the Niger Delta region, with a special focus on environmental and human degradation. In *Maters of the Moment*, set against the era of military dictatorship, issues of human rights violations, wanton corruption and flagrant abuse of power inform the narrative. In both novels, Ojaide presents rebellion as the most viable option open to the citizens. He creates heroes who embark on a process of conscience reawakening in order to mobilize the citizens to dislodge their oppressors.

Drawing from Michel Foucault's theorization of power and resistance, this essay contends that in the face of oppression, an abused and subjugated people develop the propensity to fight back. One of their weapons is literature (as knowledge and cultural practice). Consequent upon this, literature and political power has had an age-long conflicting relationship. Thus, I shall examine Ojaide's poetics of dissidence in *The Activist* and *Matters of the Moment,* but will first set a historical context by giving brief attention to the relationship between literature and power in Nigeria.

Nigerian Literature and the Institution of Power

Nigerian, nay African, writers have consistently responded to the socio-political condition of their country. This has led some critics to argue that African literature is too political or sociological (Egya 11). However, the very foundation of African literature warrants that writers respond to the political and social forces at work in the society. As Ngugi maintains, "writers are a product of history, of time and space" (12), as such they respond to the experiences that surround them. Soyinka also avers that "the artist has always functioned in African society as the record of the mores and experiences of his society and as the voice of vision in his own time" (20). For Soyinka, the artist is a chronicler and a crusader, keeping record of experiences and championing the aspirations of his society. This 'functional' role of literature leads Ojaide to proclaim that "there is, culturally speaking, no art for art's sake in Africa. Every literary work has a social function. Songs, prayers, chants, and abuse are placed at the service of the community. This utilitarian function is imbibed by modern writers" (*Poetic*14).

Indeed, Nigerian literature, since the colonial days, has been at the vanguard of protest against injustice and oppression. Ojaide's comment further encapsulates the commitment:

My generation has not been given any latitude as what it may write on. The age itself has conditioned our responses to it. We must attack with our pens one of two demons; corrupt civilian and military dictators. Literature might be devoted to pleasure in other cultures, but for us Africans who are experiencing the second half of the twentieth century, literature must serve a purpose: to expose, embarrass and fight corruption and authoritarianism. Literature has to draw attention to increasing gap between the haves and the have-nots literature has become a weapon against the denial of human rights. In the 1960s and 1970s the focus was on political corruption, which was destroying the very fabric of good governance. In the 1980s and now, socio-economic concerns have become dominant. Housing, food, health, and other basic needs which were taken for granted in the 1950s and early 1960s have become the focus of attention. (*Poetic* 125)

From this purview, Nigerian literature has instituted itself as a counter-discourse to narratives of constituted power: narratives of colonial domination, political misrule and military interventionism, for instance. The writer pitches his tent with the people against despotic leaders. As an example of what Egya calls "a discursive combat" (24), the writer uses his art as an instrument to achieve mobility towards a better society. This is where I locate Ojaide's *The Activist* and *Matters of the Moment*. By presenting a discourse of rebellion against environmental and human devastation in *The Activist* and military suppression in *Matters of the Moment*, Ojaide brings to focus the concept of power as parallel and not linear. Meaning that power is not only located within oppressive institutions of governance, but the oppressed also possess powers which they could utilize in order to challenge and dislodge their oppressors.

Michel Foucault's theorizing of power in *History and Sexuality* (1986) and *Discipline and Punish* (1991) is very useful in this context. Foucault understood power as being everywhere, diffused and embodied in 'discourse,' 'knowledge' and 'regimes of truth.' He declares that power "comes from below (too); there is no binary and all compassing opposition between the rulers and the ruled at the root of power relation" (94). By this, Foucault challenges the idea that power is wielded only by specific groups or parties, through acts of domination or coercion. Instead, he sees it as "dispersed" and "pervasive" and in a constant state of flux and negotiations, which implies that the ruled can wield power too.

A key point about Foucault's approach to power is that it transcends politics and sees power as an everyday, socialized and embodied phenomenon. Foucault explains power as both repressive and enabling. It is not just a negative, coercive or repressive thing; it can also be a necessary productive and positive force. It is a relationship that inheres in all discourses: economic, media, familial educational, religious and so on. Foucault avers that discourse can be a site of both power and resistance. He states that "discourse transmits and produces power; it reinforces it, but it also undermines and exposes it, renders it fragile and makes it possible to thwart" (*History* 100). Indeed, resistance, for Foucault is an inextricable part of power. For "when there is power, there is resistance, and yet, this resistance is never in a position of exteriority in relation to power" (*History* 95). However, for resistance to counter power, the power of resistance has to be disseminated in order to constitute a "regime of truth" (accepted forms of knowledge and truth). And, for this to be achieved, LaBranche, following Foucault, explains that there has to be a crucial maneuver to constitute a discourse regime, through knowledge and culture, that will get the oppressed people thinking and acting in the desired way (222).

Literature offers one way of constructing discourses of resistance. A writer may choose to imbue her narrative with repulsive metaphors in describing the oppressors. The writer may also infuse aggressiveness in the characters' utterances in order to stimulate the revolutionary spirit that is needed for the masses to confront their oppressors. The whole idea is to circulate and reinforce a discourse regime that will oppose the institution of power. Nigerian literature, to a large extent, responds to oppressive use of political power, its impact on the nation and the potentiality for resistance among the oppressed people. In *The Activist* and *Matters of the Moment,* Ojaide has orchestrated events of exploitation and domination into narratives that champion resistance and eventual triumph of the masses.

Environmental Activism in *The Activist*

The Activist centres on the phenomenon of oil production in Nigeria's Niger Delta. The exploitation of natural resources, the depletion of the ecosystem and the degradation of human life are the dominant themes in the novel. Ojaide chronicles yet another phase of imperialism perpetuated in the Niger Delta -

the neo-colonial politics of mineral rights- which the late Saro-Wiwa calls "a re-colonization of the region by the joint forces of the multinational oil companies and the Nigerian government" (12). The novel calls attention to the deprivation, criminality and the violence occasioned by long years of exploitation of the Niger Delta by multinational companies in collaboration with the Nigerian ruling class. It also reveals the peoples' plight and struggles through peaceful and violent means. Ojaide maintains that the militancy and criminality that overwhelms the Niger Delta are the convergent point of disenchantments that emerged mainly as a result of the exclusion of the majority by the powerful few.

Ojaide's ultimate aim in *The Activist* is perhaps to show the way that the Niger Delta could upturn her lot through activism, evident in the exploit of the hero: an American-trained academic who returns home, committed to change the order of things. His foray into politics, eventual ascension to the position of the state governor and the positive changes he brings to the state can at best be seen as the author's attempt at raising consciousness on the malevolent practices of the multinational oil companies as well as pointing an alternative to repressive leadership. Indeed, he corroborates this stance when he says elsewhere that: "as a writer, I have devoted my creative work to exposing the extent and perils of what the oil companies have been doing in the Niger Delta in order to stir awareness so that immediate action can be taken to save the Niger Delta communities, the flora and fauna, and humankind from this new scourge" (*Oil, Globalization* 3). This is the sensibility he brings to the narrative which revolves around The Activist, the hero and co- narrator whom, upon return to the Delta from the USA, commits to addressing the malaises that abound in the fictional Niger Delta state.

He is appalled by the quantum of destruction of land and waters. In a boat ride with his companion, he sadly observes that "the region now possesses a new and ugly face different from the once pristine visage" (*The Activist* 46). The river is desolate; fishes no longer inhibit the waters. Instead, river ports (by the small towns) that used to be famous for fishing "now display big boats powered by Yamaha engines" that offload varieties of frozen fish. (*The Activist* 101). Ocean supertankers that lift oil discharge sludges that contaminate the water. Oil leakages from haphazardly laid oil pipes pollute the land. Pere, the chief of the Egba boys, captures the level of destruction in this speech to his comrades:

The air used to be cool because of constant rain and the luxuriant forest, but oil licks, blowouts, and gas flares had destroyed that life. Even the rain that fell was so soot-black that no more did anybody drink rainwater, which of all waters, used to be described as God-given water. The people had lost their green and lush refuge as well. Their forest used to have deep green and lush foliage, the pride of the tropics, but that have changed, since fires often followed oil and gas accidents. *(The Activist* 82)

As a result of pollution, clean water and fresh food are scarce, leading tomalnutrition and disease.Female members of the communities observe early menstruation and menopause while men suffer sterility.

Besides the perilous state of their physical wellbeing, the people also suffer economic exploitation and harassment from security agencies. The oil companies employ local women to clean the floors for stipends; and young female graduates, selected for their physique, are made to serve tea and perform other "unofficial" services to the expatriates. Educated locals like Denise Ishaka, who are qualified for the job, are kept in the dark about the main drilling activities. The alienation of the majority goes unimpeded with the aid of some greedy local chiefs and elite who collude with the companies for financial gratification. Where the people dare to protest against the oil companies, local chiefs and elite, like Professor Tabore, Bell Oil's liaison officer, are always at hand to dissuade them. The police and military also come in to disperse peaceful demonstrations using tear gas, rubber bullets, and life ammunition in extreme cases (*The Activist* 251). Faced with these challenges, The Activist allies with Ebi, Pere and Omagbemi to dislodge the oppressors.

Ebi represents the active role of women in the rebellion.She shows concerned about the exploitation of the women of the Niger Delta by Bell oil. She reflects on how the company hires, illiterate women, for very low wages, to clean toilets and floors of the offices; and they recruit female graduates, picked for their beauty, to serve tea and meet other unofficial needs of the company's expatriates (*The Activist* 209). As part of the alliance with The Activist, she founds the Women of the Niger Delta Forum which stages nude protests in an effort to call the attention of Bell Oil and the government concerning the dangers of the company's toxic waste and gas flares on their health and environment.

Another ally of The Activist is Pere, "chief of Area boys." Pere represents the angry youth who feel alienated from the wealth that surrounds them. He is a school drop-out, a motor park tout, a thief, an armed robber, a kidnapper and an ex- convict. The novel describes him as a young man of "unpleasant disposition, given to fiery anger, impatient and irascible" (*The Activist* 73). He grew up poor; rejected by his father having lost his mother at an early age. He is angry at the society which has made some people rich while others languish in poverty. He is particularly angry at those "outsiders," those living at the expense of the "owners of the land." As a result of these, he has resolved to make them pay for making life hard for him and his kind. By kidnapping expatriates, Pere and his group wrest money from the oil companies to procure weapons which they use in making business difficult for the companies (*The Activist* 76).

Nevertheless, Pere proves to be an important ally of The Activist considering his immense contribution to the actualization of his goal. Perhaps the author is, in this instance, making a statement on the inevitability of militancy in the Niger Delta struggle, as stated, in Pere's speech to his fellow area boys: "if you add the knowledge of the university teachers to the militancy of the students, including the cultists, we will have a formidable force to move the two mountains of the military government and the multinationals" (*The Activist* 194). However, it is also an attestation to the view, as espoused by Foucault, that power resides everywhere: with the cultists, the area boys, the intellectuals, just as it resides with the military and the big corporations.

The combination of the area boys, the cult group and the women organization forms The Activist's emancipation force. Together, they use various strategies public awareness, demonstrations and protests, holding company workers under siege and lynching traitors. Their struggle pays off with the overthrow of the oppressive military regime and the enthronement of civil rule. The Activist and his army of supporters launch a formidable campaign which eventually leads to his election as the executive governor of the state- a position that empowers him to address those issues he has fought for. The story ends with the major changes he brings to the state: "he created a ministry of Environmental and Mineral Matters to deal with the problems of environmental pollution and to harness its natural resources" *(The Activist* 318). He also establishes the Niger Delta Oil Corporation and encourages the people to work towards developing their own economy rather than depending on foreigners. It is on this note that Ojaide ends his story with a liberated, healthy and wealthy Niger Delta giving opportunities to all.

Challenging Dictatorship in *Matters of the Moment*

Matters of the Moment is slightly different from *The Activist* in the sense that it takes on a national, rather than a regional concern. The novel tells the story of a country under siege by its rulers. Freedom of expression is under threat. The press is gagged, media houses are closed, journalists are harassed and detained and a bomb concealed in a parcel kills an editor.

At the same time, the nation suffers from corruption and infrastructural decay. There is constant power cut, bad roads, poor communication service. Corruption permeates the society (the government, the civil service and the private sector). Fraudulent financial organizations defraud gullible citizens; the police harass and extort commuters, and government officials embezzle public funds wantonly. Here again, Ojaide's hero is an American-trained media expert with a graduate degree in public communication. A very idealistic man, Dede Dero returns home determined to confront the despotic military regime. He takes up a poorly paid job at the federal ministry of information, instead of a well-paid one in an oil company, due to his determination to make "meaningful contribution to his society." However, the ineptitude in the civil service frustrates him until he is sacked for refusing to do the work of others who only turn up to receive salaries at the month end.

Dede gets another job at *The African Patriot,* a privately owned media house. It is there that he uses his popular column, "Matters of the Moment," to expose the ills in the society with the hope of instigating the people to challenge the regime. He also freelances for international papers like *Time Magazine*, where his essay under a pseudonym, exposes how African military rulers destroy their countries. This makes him a target of the notorious General Ogiso, leader of the Nigerian military junta.

General Ogiso, coming in the fashion of many African military rulers, promises to save the nation from civilian ravage, but he plunges the country deeper into despair. He rules the nation with an iron fist, clamping down on opposition and eliminating dissenting voices. The people live in fear, for the General is said to have ears to the ground. But Dede continues his assault on the General, exposing the illegality of military rule, describing it as "an aberration and an affront to humanity and civilization" *(Matters* 42). He challenges the military on embezzlement, youth unemployment, poverty and extra-judicial execution. His column insists that the country is "so brutalized that it was sick and dying and emergency measures had to be taken to avert its end" *(Matters 78).* For his consistent "embarrassment" of the government, he is arrested and detained along with his editor.

Dede realizes that he alone cannot make his dream, "to rattle the leopard and bring down the military government with his pen" *(Matters 127)*, come true. So he seeks alliance. He reaches out to university students. Even though his planned lecture is banned by the authorities, texts from his speech is circulated and pasted around the campus, stirring the spirit of revolt. He also attends the meeting of the disabled people and delivers a moving speech aimed at provoking them to join the resistance against military domination. Dede joins the National Forum for Democracy, a coalition of civil organizations demanding the General to step aside and allow civil rule. The forum, in collaboration with the labor unions, organizes a national strike that grounds the nation for an entire week. The strike culminates in a grand street march by the disabled, the labor unions, students, pro-democracy groups to the presidency.

General Ogiso does not survive to witness the people's insurrection. In a rather complicated twist, he dies in his mistress' bed. Franka Udi, Minister of Information and Culture and Dede's estranged wife, has risen to prominence as a result of her escapades with top military men in the Junta. Her affair with General Ogiso lands her the ministerial job. As the General dies in her bed, she is afraid for her life, she covers up his death and runs the country for days while she figures out an escape route. The day Ogiso's body is discovered coincides with the peoples' great march. As the protesters advance, more people join them "and the crowed became a swell of population." Even the soldiers throw away their guns and uniforms and join the protesters for fear of being lynched (*Matters,* 181). The people's triumphant march sends shivers down the spines of the military echelon, and no one dares to assume the position of the despised despot. An interim committee is set up to prepare for general elections. At the end, it is victory for the people.

Conclusion

In the final analysis, Ojaide's *Matters of the Moment* and *The Activist* are similar in a number of ways. There is a concern with historicity as both novels respond to real experiences the Nigerian nation underwent - oil exploration in the Niger Delta and military dictatorship in the nation. Both novels depict the plight of the people. Both novels demonstrate the positive use of power; a use of power for justice and equity. This attest to Foucault's call that: "we must cease once and for all to describe the effects of power in negative terms…in fact, power produces; it produces reality; it produces domains of objects and rituals of truth. The individual and the knowledge that maybe gained of him belong to this production" (*Discipline* 194).

The heroes in the novels and the knowledge that they disperse, which leads to the desired change, are all products of power: a positive use of power that dethrones oppressive power. In *The Activist,* democracy is restored and the people have a say in their affairs. In *Matters of the Moment,* the junta is dislodged, and a process is set for democratic elections. *The Activist* and *Matters of the Moment* demonstrate the people's will and power to resistance and change. Ojaide shows that the people can rise above their peripheral status and also wield power. His novels indicate that fiction holds the potential, however unconsciously, to depict a peoples' knowledge and perception, and get them to exercise the power which they also possess.

Works Cited

Achebe, Chinua. "The Black Writer's Burden" *Presence Africaine* Vol. 59. 1966 133-40.

Egya, Sule E. *Nation, Power, and Dissidence in Third Generation Nigerian Poetry in English.*
    Unisa University Press, 2014.

Foucault, Michel. *The History of Sexuality, Volume 1: An Introduction.* Trans. Robert Hurley.
   Penguin, 1986.

—-. *Discipline and Punish: The Birth of a Prison.* Penguin, 1991.

Ngugi, Wa. Thiong'o. *Writers in Politics: A Re-Engagement with issues of Literature and Society.* James Curry, 1997.

Ojaide, Tanure. *The Activist.* Farafina Press, 2006.

… *Matters of The Moment.* Malthouse Press Limited, 2009.

…*Poetic Imagination in Black African: Essays on African Poetry.* Durham Academic
  Press, 1986.

Saro-Wiwa, Ken. *A Month and A Day London.* Penguin Books, 1995.

Soyinka, Wole. "The Writer in a Modern African State": Art, Dialogue and Outrage.
Essays on Literature and Culture. New Horn, 1988, 15-36.

Marxism and Tanure Ojaide's Social Vision

Adama Haruna Idrisu

Ojaide's shift from the Euro-modernist style of the old poets to Marxism is conditioned by the appropriate nature of the ideology which best demonstrates his social vision and more in consonance with the African folkloric genre. His concern with the liberation of the downtrodden from any form of domination is central to the Marxist principles. Ojaide's mounting aspiration is to conscientize the people whose attitude, belief and class consciousness have been shaped by the general or prevailing ideology of the ruling class. According to Lois Althusser, "the dominant class imposes its ideology on the proletariat and this makes them to accept their condition as ideal" (Bressler: 217). Faced with these varied dimensional challenges, it becomes imperative for Ojaide to contend with the urgent socio-economic problems on one hand and reorient the mindset of the masses on the other hand. The urgency of the new experience necessitated the utilization of people-oriented language to urgently communicate and consceientize the masses more effectively. The corrupt and inefficient leadership portrayed in many of his poetry collections, expose the awkward relationship between the rulers and the ruled, which are oppression, exploitation and deprivation. Ojaide's portrayal of these anomalies is in line with the Marxist aesthetic.

The inefficient leadership and corruption affect the living condition of the masses and forms his social vision. His concern with the predicament of the masses is responsible for the presentation of his thematic features: socio-economic problems and especially their consequences on the masses from the Marxist perspective. His opposition of the ruling class is in consonance with the Marxist basic principle of:

Opposition to an economic system based on the inequality and exploitation of the majority (by means of the system of wage labour), a system whose purpose is to obtain profits for some people rather than satisfying the needs of all. This describes capitalism […] (Critique Sociale: March 21st 2009).

In Ojaide's presentation of his social vision from the Marxist perspective, his authorial ideology opposes the general ideology of the neo-colonialists, but it agrees with the Marxist principles, which stand against inequality, exploitation, fragmentation and repression. In Steven Lynn's view, relevant Marxist literary works identify "who is being oppressed and exploited and by whom?" (Lynn: 131). Louis Althusser reiterates that "the people's world view is craftily shaped by the message sent", (Bressler: 217) through the superstructure. The poet is however, optimistic that literary work is the only weapon that can overthrow the bourgeois dominance and by portraying their oppressive tendencies, corruption and social injustice, it will reorient the mindset of the masses in consonance with the assertion that "some of the damages caused by the economics of capitalism, according to Marxists is psychological (Doble: 83). In Ojaide's attempt to conscientize the masses, he doggedly maintains his stance and continued to publish one collection of poetry after another with the aim of achieving this objective. This endeavor has also elevated Ojaide's reputation on the literary scene and among his contemporaries, thereby making him the "most prolific of the generation of Nigerian writers after the Soyinka" (Okome: 9) group.

Ojaide is concerned with the environmental degradation of the Niger-Delta resulting from the oil exploration by the multi-national companies. This is the focal points in the collection entitled *Delta Blues and Homesongs*. In the poem, titled "When Green was the Lingua Franca," for instance, the poet gives a contrastive view of the Niger-Delta landscape, before and after the devastation caused by the gas flaring, which has brought negative changes in the economic history of the region. The poet captures the virgin land of the Niger-Delta with its rich vegetation ("forest green"), when the "water sparkles…" with purity and the "snails", "koto" ("a snail-shell used in children's game" (Shija: 164) "urhurhu" and "owe apple" lured him as a child "to defy every distance" to pick. The presence of "Ikere froglets" and the "skipper-fish" confirm the richness of the flora and fauna of the rain forest before the disruption of the growth and continuity of organic life (Bodunde:198); that followed the activities of the multi-national companies:

The Ethiope waterfront
wiped out by prospectors
so many trees beheaded
and the streams mortally poisoned
in the name of job and wealth! (13).

Ojaide refers to Shell Oil Company "as the symbol of devastation, the monster that "broke the bond/with quakes and a hell/of flare" (Bodunde: 198). The "unbroken park" of green trees ends up as the personified "victims of arson". Some of the "trees beheaded" could no longer provide that "tropical sheet". The streams were equally "mortally poisoned/in the name of job and wealth!", but ironically poverty turns out to be the anticipated "job and wealth". The "green forest" then became "the desert advancing land". The poet thus confesses that "for fear of being counted" among the "mad ones," he refused" "…to plant trees/ beyond … (his) fenced compound"(14). Ojaide personifies the trees when he says "I left the majority to be/massacred, a tearful carnage" and it portrays his emotional state. The fruits from the trees not only provide nourishment but the amputated "leaves and weed" serve as healing herbs. Shija describes the devastation meant for the creation of "jobs and wealth" as a transformation in the "productive activities from the agrarian culture to an industrialized one. A new society has been born which according to the Marxist belief in linear progress of history is inevitable" (Shija: 167-8).

The subject of environmental degradation re-surfaces in "Delta Blues". In this poem Ojaide cries out that the "delta of birth" with its "evergreen leaves" and "home of plants and birds" has been transformed into "Barrels of alchemical drought". The air and water pollution and the devastation of the landscape for the 'profit-drive' of the oil companies causes "immortal pain": "My nativity gives immoral pain/ Masked in barrels of oil. (21).

The extraction of the "barrels of oil" is responsible for the deathless pain and Ojaide broods amidst plenty "in the deathbed" of poverty "prepared by a cabal of brokers"; "a paradox of hunger in the middle of feasting" (Bodunde: 202). The prospectors did not only impoverish the soil and its people by "tainting ... a thousand rivers ... /... but the idea of scorching the air and soil" is the aftereffect of their activities. They also transferred the people's birthright into a "boon cake for others". The "money mongers" are also responsible for breaking the serenity and destroying the hospitable environment that once played host to even birds and animals, thereby driving them to the sea and the hinterland: "My birds take flight to the sea/ The animals grope in burning bushes,/ Head blindly to the hinterland." (22). Subsequently, the poet presents "through indirect allusions [...] the dialectical structuring of the two classes engaged in the struggle" (Shija: 175) with the oil prospectors, ruling class on one hand and the exploited people on the other. He describes the dominant class as "baron robbers,'" "uniformed dogs" are "barking and biting" while the masses brandish only "green shrubs in protest". Ojaide links the oil resources to Olukun's benediction and reveals how they disappointed her by bidding: "good–bye to ... (their) birth right,/ now a boon cake for others".

The poet thus ponders on how the sea goddess and giver of wealth, Olukun, will "look at her beneficiaries/dead or still living in the racks ...?" He, however, blames "relatives" or kinsmen who are supposed to serve as "standard bearers" but betrayed their trust to exploiters who are "careless for the minority rights" as he says: "The standard bearer's betrayed/ in the house by thieves, relatives ...?" Greed also serves as one of the reasons for societal fragmentation as the relatives exhibit.

Ojaide portrays the relationship between the ruler and ruled through the peaceful approach of the Niger-Delta people to inform military leaders of their predicament in the poem "Season". There is a contrast between the peaceful approach of the masses and violent response of the military. While they take the path of dialogue, the military scares them with guns: "we selected delegates to take our prayers to Abuja/but the guns scared them...". In a nutshell, the ruling class is supporting the bourgeoisie to become richer at the expense of the deprived people of the Niger-Delta, who are becoming poorer. The attitude of the ruling class is not suprising because the neo-colonialists are also their allies. Phyllis Goldberg reveals that the African bourgeoisie "...are hegemonic over the miserable masses, but depend on the international bourgeoisie" (Ojaide and Obi: 18) to perpectuate their domination. The use of guns to scare the people also indicates how the military that is part of the superstructure, is used in suppressing the masses. Using a rhetorical question the poet inquires: "If you took fins from a fish, would it be fish?" The removal of the fins from a fish symbolizes a 'systematic elimination' or rather segregation against his people and thus societal fragmentation:

The irony that confronts the underprivileged in the second section lies in their attempt to kill the "pythons ... (they) believed meant evil," but they do not remember "nursing cobras in ... (their) closets". This means that the enemy within, which is the ruling class, is worse than the external imperial power they are trying to destroy. The oppressive leaders are thus presented as "trickster–cannibals", "vultures" and "hyena'" which are all symbols of murderous creatures and images of the exploitative. Ojaide also attributes the situation to moral decadence that has consumed the nation such that even the "priests no longer know the god they worship". In a nation where the religious leaders, who are supposed to uphold the light of truth and serve as models to the people exhibit the contrary, the perpetration of evil will no doubt become the norm.

Ojaide depicts the high level of corruption in Nigerian courts, where a thief can sue anyone who addresses him as a thief for defamation of character because "he knows the courts are on sale" and he will secure undeserved justice: "When you call a thief a thief, he grins and sues/ you for libel! he knows the courts are on a sale;/ police and lawyers wait for litigants in hallways" (15). The police and lawyers are not different. He likens them to the "vultures" and this implies that they are also corrupt and deprived, because they do not have clients like "vultures overseeing a desolate country". In essence, the poet is saying that it is not only the ruling class ("hyena") who are corrupt but the judiciary, police and lawyers are corrupt such that they can grant any rich client (thieves inclusive) undeserved justice. Ojaide is actually saying that the poor people of Niger-Delta can not access justice even if they present their exploitation case before the court of law. Ironically justice that is supposed to be for everyone excludes the masses, it is only for the rich.

Unlike some of the kinsmen who betrayed the people's trust, Ken Saro-Wiwa whose memory the poet invokes in "Delta Blues" is seen as the symbol of resistance in the struggle before his execution alongside the eight Ogoni leaders by the military dictator General Sani Abacha. The death of the warriors created a conflict between the ruling class/bourgeoisie and the aggrieved masses. The rebellious youths developed the courage and resolved to advance the cause, for which the human rights died. The second section of "elegy for the nine warriors" depicts the decision of the youths:

We'll surely find a way in the dark

that covers and cuts us from those waiting

to raise the white and green flag to the sky.

The eagle nests in the nursery of advancing days

we'll find a way to reach there

where the chorus rehearses celebratory chant

we'll make our way in the dark

but would have lost the fear in our hearts

the dark will not close eyes

to knowledge of stars, dawn and sun, (28).

The repetitive use of the first person plural pronoun "we" signifies a collective consensus to reach the goal set by the martyrs, a just cause that claimed their lives. The youths proclaim their preparedness to grope in the dark till they "raise the white and green flag" of triumph for the others who are waiting. In their exhibition of confidence, the uncertainty that they express initially transforms into a declaration of assurance: "we'll find a way to reach there… /we'll make a way in the dark". Their position is more defined as they become resolute to make their "way in the dark". They believe the darkness is short-lived as it must give way to a new "dawn and sun" of brilliant days ahead, "where the chorus rehearses celebratory chant". The youths acknowledge the dangers "of ambush of hangmen/who do not commit their eyes/to sleep…" but they are undaunted:

We'll find a way to reach there

Without government road or light

but with the rage of being held back

from what we can grasp, stretching ourselves

to the point of exhaustion or death.

None of the survivors will then be

ashamed of being afraid. (29).

The youths' resolution to reach their goal is anchored on their "rage" of being denied what legitimately belongs to them: "the rage of being held back/from what we can grasp". They equally accept to be exhausted or even die ("stretching ourselves/ to the point of exhaustion or death") trying to achieve their objective. Though they believe that some of them might lose their lives in the process, they nevertheless feel that the "survivors will (not) then be /ashamed of being afraid". The conflict between the ruling class / bourgeoisie and the masses is often due to unequal distribution of goods (wealth) and services, which is central to Marxist principles of existence. The conflict between the two social classes, typifies what Marxism and African folkloric genre share. The presentation of small animals as trickish, while the bigger ones are depicted as foolish, to the extent the smaller animals triumph over them is an attribute of oral tradition, a concept which Ojaide deploys. In like manner, Marxism supports the weak to triumph over the strong which is the meeting point of African oral tradition and Marxism.

Ojaide in the same section chips in Nigeria's lack of social amenities such as "roads and light", which are not only central in the development of many nations but essential to industrialization and trade. Though exploited the people of the Niger-Delta are deprived of amenities necessary for their well-being. He also captures the road condition and how the "waterways" are clogged thereby making traveling by road and water ways difficult: "Roads became a string of potholes./ Water hyacinths closed waterway for boats." (51).

Ojaide also presents the "upright clan of diviners," who detest crime in the poem titled "Exception". Being upright they dread corruption and these are the category of people that the emperor enjoys persecuting:

> The emperor persecutes the upright clan of diviners
> whose words ring ominous bells for power-play
> if only they would be gods whose mouths closed with food.
> He will stuff them to their necks with national cake
> baked with the same oil that incinerated gun heads
> but these would not taste forbidden food that invite the word.
> Even if it meant they starved and fought with bones
> they preferred being black ants stinging his buttocks
> borne by the high stool that's daily daubed with blood
> the executive of the vast domain of servants and prisoners. (49).

The emperor persecutes the upright because of their ideological stance. Ojaide sarcastically describes Abatcha as an "emperor" because of his ambition to succeed himself. Unlike some elite, who compromised theirs conscience for monetary gains, the mouths of the upright can not be closed with food or wealth ("national cake"), because they "hate the taste of forbidden food", (fruits of corruption). "They prefer to be black ants stinging his buttocks" and to disturb his peace, which will make him uncomfortable despite the attempt to secure his "stool that's daily daubed with blood". The leader is portrayed as the "executive of the vast domain of servants and prisoners", which characterizes his dictatorial trait.

Although Ojaide highlights the upright to serve as paragon, he condemns the proletariat that brings about fragmentation among the masses. Some of the reasons that brings about societal fragmentation is also evident in the poem "In Our Time". Ojaide deploys the concept of stigmatization of bastard children as the cause of drought from the oral rendition. This belief was employed to caution and instill morals into the younger generation. As a result drought problems were countered through organized communal sacrifice to appease the gods, which in turn induced rainfall. The poet is, however, not in support of this belief and Anne Doble states that an "ideology supports or subverts the power structure it addressees" (Doble: 88). Such children do not only suffer from the stigma associated with this belief, but they are also resented and segregated. The poet thus deploys this belief and relates it to the circumstances surrounding such birth:

> In our time
> they say bastard children cause the unending drought
> but we raised them on dehydrated breast
> tied pebble as charms round their necks.
> Weak from birth, they were safe nowhere.
> There was no dew to cleanse them

before sunrise, no mist on their way;
they for saw their end from the first cry (28).

The poet rejects the belief that bastards are responsible for the "unending drought "by stating that they are also victims of the drought as their mothers "raised (them) on dehydrated breasts" and they have been "weak from birth", which is an indication of hunger. The pebble tied round their neck as charms could probably be to ward off the malediction surrounding their birth. The lack of "dew" and "mist" in lines six and seven of the poem symbolize poverty, the hopeless condition of bastards which the poet presents as he declares "they saw their end from the first cry" (beginning). The poet extends the idea of their hopelessness into the ninth and tenth lines through a rhetorical question thus: "what awaited them other than the same dust/that already inflicted their genes?" He also describes the kind of fate and life they were born into: "The only excitement they knew was war,/ Thrust upon them by unknown parents/ Fighting shy of obscenities." (28).

Stigma, discrimination and resentment have reduced these children into "scape-goat of the society" (Shija: 108). Based on these problems, they neither "bleed when they trip on stones", nor do they "… have tear to shed in pain". This means that they have been forced into silence by society's discrimination and contempt. In like manner, the relationship between the ruling class and the masses is a replica of the one that exists between the bastards and the people of their community. Society is thus divided against itself. The ruling class does not only discriminate against the masses, they also silence them like the way the stigmatized bastards have been driven back into their shell from birth: "they were safe nowhere". Ojaide, however, deploys this belief in order to ridicule the ruling class, because the illegitimate children are better than them. While the children "do not groan aloud in their racks/among a people who relish the spectacles of sacrifice," the oppressors cannot offer "their own blood or comfort" to induce rain, which symbolizes a blessing that integrates all.

The fragmentation of or discrimination against the downtrodden of any society has long been part of human behavior. Every society has a particular group of people they look down upon. This has been a practiced before the European incursion. Societal fragmentation negates the Marxist principle, that is why Marxism encourages the proletariat to develop their own literature to counter the bourgeois ideas, which is disseminated through the superstructure. Ojaide in the poem "In Our Time", depicts the fundamental problem of the society by cautioning the underprivileged that fragmentation is the great divide between them and their goal of overthrowing the ruling class.

Ojaide again portrays grave consequences of environmental degradation in the poem "Libation". (*When It No Longer Matters Where You Live*). This problem of economic retrogression in the Niger-Delta derives from the activities of the oil-prospectors. The aftermath of the exploration created man-made desertification and the pollution of both air and water, thereby driving fishes from the river and animals from the destroyed forest as well. The poet, however, blames the ruling class in Abuja for these situations: "And the bees of Abuja wreak havoc on the public/ Without benefit of enjoying their droughts" (39). The adverse effect of the pollutions are many:

> the grubs emanciate in the groins of the palm
> the tadpoles of the hurricane season are stunted
> in a dry bed; departed, milk from coconut
> the droves of fish abandon the rivers and soup pots
> the migrant birds disorientated forget their homes. (39).

The poet describes the ruling class as "bees of Abuja" that deprive the masses from "enjoying their draughts". The metaphoric presentation of the "flora and fauna" results from "the incapacitation of the Niger-Delta" (Olaoluwa: 181). Consequently, the "grubs emanciate" "tadpoles" suffer stunted growth, coconut is devoid of milk, while "fish abandon (the) rivers" and "birds … forget their homes" because of pollution and "the bush flares". The resultant effect is that "fishers and hunters return" home with neither fish nor game. The gas flaring also deprives the farmer of harvest as "the sack folds without storage of corn or millet". The metaphoric presentation of Nigeria shrinking "into a mole" and its populace into "dunes of dry leaves" reveals the extent of it is impoverishment and death. Ojaide describes the period of military dictatorship as "days of shriveling hardship" and labels Nigeria as "a nation of thieves". He ponders who will liberate the "sacred ground that's bloodstained?" The desecration of the "sacred ground" is due to the human sacrifice and the execution of the nine warriors which the poet repeatedly refers to in many of the poems in the collection entitled *Delta Blues and Homesongs*. Other consequences of the flaring inferno are:

> The trap rusts from oxidizing wind
> babies slump from back of mothers
> the cassava farms are gone with drought
> beggars mob the street with disabled spirit
> they dangle the stumps of their executed hopes
> now drowned in undammed waves of tears (39).

The poet enumerates the victims of the 'economic emasculation' of the nation as innocent babies that slump to death on "back of mothers", farmers that lose their produce ("cassava farms") to man-made drought and beggars that throng the streets, thrusting mutilated hands and bereft of hope, they are "drowned ... in waves of tears" of poverty. The poet further shows how the economic crises cause sicknesses and death among the peasants: "How many deaths from sickness come/ from rusty plates and scurvies mouths?" (40). The use of rusty plates describes the extent of deprivation and penury, which results into poisoning ailments and death. The massive demise of the masses has mandatorily converted the "farms and dry streams" into cemeteries. Other neighbouring nations empathize with the dead and the walking-corpses: "the dying (who) have lost direction". The paradox of a rich oil-nation and especially the Niger-Delta that is endowed with the wealth that Nigeria depends on, "is ironically typified by poverty" (Olaoluwa: 181) as "the people are herded into holes / (and they) suffer the suffocating smoke of want". This is an indication of inhuman treatment in addition to the "stifling poverty". Ojaide, however, believes that the fate of the ruler is uncertain: with "one leg lost in the deeps, the other hanging to the land/the fate of the elephant hangs in the air". On account of the "running blood", the world is clamoring for the murderer's removal, but the Niger-Delta people remain passive without any attempts at freeing themselves: "but my people still fold their arms, wait/ for reprieve without massing out from cells". The image of an insatiable glutton is what the ruler represents as he syphones the public funds meant to provide social services to the populace. The nation is compelled to retrogress developmentally and pushing us back to what the poet describes as "an antiquated millennium".

"In a Search for a Fresh Song". Ojaide presents a 'graphic vision' of poverty, as it affects the Niger-Delta masses, which is also the after-effect of environmental degradation. He shows how their social condition of living, has diminished to an unimaginable proportion because of hunger and the filthy environment breeds diseases and death:

The afflicted neighborhood – damp, sour air
that disperses death in the isolated ward.
I have witnessed bloated feet wade naked
through this slush of unlettered street
everywhere unrinary, toilet or vast spittoon;
I faced sweat-logged wraiths as easily knock
down by motor-bikes as by fever and want.
(44).

The stench of filth pervades the air and "disperses death in the isolated ward" of the downtrodden. Among the suffering masses is one with "bloated feet" trudging with difficulty through mire "of unlettered street" infested with "urine, toilet and vast spittoon". The reference to the unlettered "street" means that the area is a slum. Some of the masses the poet observes are "sweat-logged wraiths" or phantom-like moving shadows that can "easily (be) knocked down by motor-bikes" as much as they are susceptible to "fever and want". The "fetid pools" of floods also breeds mosquitoes that cause malaria parasites which inflict the people with fever. The rusted pots indicates poverty ("dearth of naira") and drinking water from such unhygienic pots can transmit the "many plagues that" they suffer and their bread appears "stale and "ever damp yet it fills a million mouths […] ?" The "graphic vision", which sores the poet's heart inspires the song which "rises out of the haunting vision". Although he wishes that the "stifling mire" of filth be destroyed, yet he asserts that the "vast net […] (has) caught so many" and worse still, "they don't even know how deep/and gone they are in the trap". This lack of consciousness to their condition affirms the view that:

The Marxist is aware that the working class does not always recognize the system in which it has been caught. The dominant class, using its power to make the prevailing system seem to be logical, natural one, entraps the proletariat into holding the sense of identity and worth that the bourgeois want them to hold, one that will allow the powerful to remain in control (Doble: 85).

The poet emphasizes the condition of the people and desire for a change in the diseased slum. Olaoluwa says "the search for environmental sanity in the famous oil city of Warri can best be compared to the search for rivers in a desert. The environmental eyesores must also be viewed as an indication of poverty compatible only with socio-economic exclusion" (Olaoluwa: 182), which is contrary to expectation, because of the economic viability of the oil rich zone.

Ojaide identifies bribery and corruption as the root of Nigeria's many problems in "Home Song: IV". Corruption he says has crippled the nation's power plants and the trodden and their siblings are the most affected as they go to bed in darkness and the heads of their children "have grown heavy", because the parents are unable to give them the informal education through folktales. Power failure has deprived people of much needed comfort to sleep deep and dream and thus Ojaide poses the rhetorical questions: "My people, when did we dream last/ On these blackout nights? (55). Ojaide thus ponders, when will the ruling class renounce their "insatiable appetite" or excessive love of material wealth? The proverb in the lines that say, "the testament of the brave is/commensurate with their power" cannot be applied to Nigeria, because despite her strength of number, size and resources, she remains a giant weakling that has to be pulled out of the abyss of corruption. Ojaide observes that Nigerians will probably be homeless within its own frontiers if the "looting riot continues". Worse still, corruption is responsible for our low rating among the Commonwealth of Nations.

The delineation of the living conditions of the lower, middle and upper class is the concern of "Home Song: IX". This classification is done to highlight the hunger-related ailments that affect the lower class. Ojaide observes that some homes have more than sufficient food to the extent that their day's desert and snacks are capable of satisfying "a hundred deficient families" and also free them from hunger-related ailments such as "kwashiorkor and beri-beri", but these homes do not extend helping hands to the needy. The protein and vitamin deficiency related ailments are the identification or "uniform" of the underprivileged class. The middle-class is also self-centered as they are depicted thus: "For those above the doomed line, there's/ no "Let's stop here midway so that others/ can continue to live on sumptuous leftovers". (67). Ojaide stresses that "Even as children, … (they) never left … (their) plates clean,/ but offered Omoyeye, the needy in the shadows,/ enough to keep him alive in the spirit world". (67), but unfortunately, this class does not believe in the act of giving charity to support the starved, let alone allow them access to their "sumptuous leftovers". The upper class which comprises of the ruling class and bourgeoisie are not only gluttonous and selfish; they arrogantly laugh at the impoverished masses, who are victims of their evil schemes: "Now those who have the hyena's secret means / Wipe off the shares of those without reach/ in the daily brawl to live on others' losses". (67). The open display of their insatiable desire for material wealth makes them to steal "the shares of those without reach" to public funds. In so doing, the poor are abandoned to starvation and diseases. To hide such loot from public knowledge, they bank their wealth and buy properties abroad. The poet ponders at their "insatiable desire" for material wealth, in addition to the gluttony that leaves "mother's pot pale before Maigida's obesity". Apart from wiping the pot clean without remembering the poor and needy, Ojaide describes them as "the cunning (that) laugh at their victims", who are "marked/by dreary uniform of kwashiorkor and beri-beri". This is an indication of heartlessness, arrogance and lack of empathy towards the plight of the trodden they repress. The reference to the ruling class not "obey(ing) traffic rules" and their ignorance of not knowing "when to stop for others to pass" simply means that the ruling class does not know when to relinquish power for others to take over. Thus the poet warns that "the gluttonous fly will be buried with the corpse". This poem affirms the Marxist assertion that the society is stratified into social classes and such unequal distribution of goods and services are responsible for class conflict.

Ojaide's concientization of the masses through his revolutionary aesthetic is evident in "Opening Song" (*When It No Longer Matters Where You Live).* He portrays the different responsibilities of a revolutionary at every stage of his growth in "Opening Song". First as a child he is expected to "run errands"; as a youth, he "wakes the community from stupor" and takes over the responsibilities of his parents:

Now that the child walks,
let him run errands for the village;
now that the cockerel's come of crowing age
let it wake the community from stupor
now that the stump's grown back into an iroko,
let it shield the forest with its crown (29).

Ojaide uses symbolism to depict the stages of the child's growth. The image of cockerel represents the stage of youthful exuberance with accompanying rebelliousness. At this "crowing age" he is expected to conscientize and wake the people from slumber. The same metaphorical "stump" used by the poet: "stump will grow into another Iroko" (19), to describe the death of the activist Saro-Wiwa in *Delta Blues and Homesongs* is sustained in this poem that is, *"Opening Song".* This signifies that another revolutionary will take over from where he (Saro-Wiwa) stopped, just as he stepped into the shoes of Boro. The stump imagery in *When It No Longer Matters Where you Live* describes the aged, whom the youth replace and provide the necessary protection for the community as the iroko tree "shield(s) the forest with its crown". The extension and repetition of stump imagery, throws more light on the "stump (that has) grown back into an iroko". In like manner Ojaide "excuses….(his) parents from the dance," to exhibits it with more vitality. This indicates that the revolutionary activity will be pursued with more vigour. Ojaide counsels the "watchman" who is also poet or the revolutionary that he should not complain of insomnia and he complains of the passivity of everyone as he writes: "Let no watchman complain of insomnia!/ No lullaby will send the crab to sleep …" (29). Ojaide feels that the "watchman" is performing his responsibility to humanity, so he should discharge it without complaining of restlessness. On his part, he confesses that "no lullaby" can make him go to sleep ("no lullaby can send the crab to sleep") and he paraphrases the above lines thus: "I cannot sleep over deep wounds, nor/can I throw the succuba, Africa's bane". What he refers to as his "deep wounds" is the pain he experiences over the destruction of Africa by its leaders. He reveals the complacency of the masses, makes him ashamed: "I am ashamed that impotence caught everyone". He thus resolves that during this "sun-racked season" he "waits for dew/to nurse the plant of freedom to fruition" but he is currently conscientizing the people through his song like the wakeful crow of the cock. Ojaide has not only reaffirmed his ideological stance of conscientizing the society through a revolutionary call but he points out that the masses are not playing their expected role. The stump image that he carries over from *Delta Blues and Homesongs* into this poem "Opening Songs", that the stump has grown back into an Iroko; signifying that the poet has taken over from where Saro-Wiwa stopped.

Ojaide confirms that he is the iroko in the poem entitled "I am still the Iroko". Although the poem opens with reference to his relocation to the United States of America, he ties this to destiny. Using the Hegelian Marxist philosophy of "the relationship of part to (a) whole (Selden: 95), Ojaide declares through an interrogative technique that he is still "part of (Nigeria's) … body" and his presence completes its missing part "for wholeness":

> Does the land
> that threw me out
> miss me like
> a part of its body
> It wants back
> for wholeness? (19).

The Hegelian philosophy of presenting society like an organism is the technique, Ojaide adopts, when he presents himself as the missing part of Nigeria's body which it needs "for wholeness". The Hegelian Marxists are of the view that every part or sector in the society is relevant for it to function adequately and so is Ojaide's role as part of Nigeria's body. He then states that probably he is "more than/a stranger to those/who don't know/… (his) green leaves". The "green leaves" symbolize his unchanging ideological stance. He emphasizes how much he has been in touch with Nigeria as he states that people who come home on vacation bring "back/songs that fill … (him) with longing to return". He reveals how he is very much part of Nigeria in these words:

> My faithful birdfriend
> brings me
> the homestead soil
> to build my own island
> within this island
> I am not caught off
> from home draughts. (20).

The idea he expresses in the first five lines of the excerpt means that he has isolated himself from his immediate abode and he psychologically feels as if the island of his isolation is, an extension of his homeland, Nigeria. This way he says, "I am not caught off/from the home draughts". By implication the poet is saying, though he is domiciles in a foreign land his main concern is his homeland and not those of his foreign home.

Ojaide explains the reason why some Nigerians flee to the western world in the poem titled "When It No Longer Matters Where You Live". The successive military regimes were characterized by 'stifling inferno' and the wailing masses "comb the breadth of the land" in search of a healer or "saviour", but ironically the messiah they found turns out to be a murderer. In a metaphorical presentation of the dictatorial leadership of the ruler, Ojaide describes him as the: "wild fires (that) have consumed bark and herbs" and he asserts that there is no certainty of capturing "the lion alive".

> Except by returning to libate the soil
> with the cock of Abuja's blood
> will exile not offend martyred ones?
> For all its refuge, the foreign home
> Remains a night whose dawn
> I wish arrives before its time (77).
> ...
> until home becomes safe to return to,
> when it no longer matters
> where you choose to live (77)

Although libation for purification is an African belief, but the solution, which Ojaide proffers to "libate the soil" is the blood of the dictatorial "cock of Abuja". Ojaide's suggestion is interrogative but the option is a difficult one, since the object of sacrifice for the purification of the land is the dictator. He then confesses that although exile serves as refuge but Ojaide expresses his dissatisfaction thus: "the foreign home/remains a night whose dawn/ (he) … wishes arrives before its time". Ojaide further asserts the pain the Nigerians in exile encounter: "There's none so hurt at home/ who forgets the pain outside/ that persistent ache one carries".

The socio-economic problems borne out of inefficient leadership and corruption are responsible for the "pain at home". These in turn engraves "the pain outside" on the memory and it is the incessant "ache one carries". This particular poem "When It No Longer Matters Where You Live" and especially the excerpt above have been the crux of controversy among critics. According to Shija, Okome, was the first to suggest "that exile seems a permanent option for Ojaide" (Shija: 205). Okome stated this after he assessed "No Longer Our Country" from *Blood of Peace and Other Poems*, and relates it to the above except as the bedrock for his argument. Okome links this message in the controversial except where he discusses the poet's lament in "No Longer Our Country" and concludes that "exile now seems a permanent option. It is inevitable... Another kind of home is fast forming...This is the profound meaning of Ojaide's new book of poems *When it No Longer Matters Where You Live"* (Okome: 15). Shija also shares Okome's view as he remarks that:

Ojaide views his home and country of exile as equally strewn with hazards. Accordingly, he notices a strange duality of fortunes, that of freedom and lack of it, joy and sorrow, happiness and tragedy all stand close together on either side of the divide. The poet juxtaposes the "refuge" in the foreign home with the uncertainty of the long "night" whose dawn is reluctant to arrive. He also compares "the hurt at home" with "the pain outside" and arrives at the conclusion that it no longer matters where anyone may choose to live in the world (210-11).

Olaoluwa on the other hand argues that:

....the entire collection lies in the concealed irony of the title...The irony that defines this title poem....gives an impression that in the age of globalization it no longer counts where people choose to live. To that extent, the first impression is a false signal about an uncritical reception of cosmopolitan ideals by the poet.

In his condemnation of Shija's interpretation, Olaoluwa asserts that:

From another angle, Shija in his essay "Exile and globalization in the poetry of Tanure Ojaide: A case study of *When it Longer Matters Where You Live"* (2008: 33) weighing both options of living at home and exile, concludes that... "Ojaide views both his home and his country of exile as equally strewn with hazards". Nevertheless, one cannot but see beyond the balance and the dilemma that such critical view as Shija creates, for the option in the end tilts towards home. Once we recognize that even at its best the "refuge" of "foreign home" remains "a night whose dawn/I wish arrives before its time" (Olaoluwa: 186).

I shares Olaoluwa's condemnation of Shija's interpretation which tallies with Okome's assertion that "another kind of home is fast forming". Undoubtedly, Shija gave an explicit reading of the section but aligns Ojaide's view to the choice of the foreign land as home. Apart from Olaoluwa's apt explanation that "the option in the end tilts towards home", Ojaide has expressed his obsession with his homeland; Nigeria in some of his poems in the collection. In the poem titled "I am still the iroko", for instance, Ojaide expresses such obsession by stressing that a "bird friend" of his brought him the "homestead's soil" to "build" his own "island/within an island"(19). The "homestead's soil" establishes a connection between him and his home country and at the same time erects a psychological barrier between him and his place of domicile abroad. In "Immigrant Voice", The poet declares his preference for Africa's sweet home to America's hell: "Sometimes I cry my eyes red for night in bed/ wetin my eye don see for here pass pepper/ make me de prepare go sweet home" (106). Ojaide condemns America's high level of crime, destitution, murder, poverty and above all, the unfriendliness of Americans that makes them live a life of isolation. Africa is, however, considered as "sweet home" in comparison with America, which he considers as "hell".

Another grave issue that critics raise about this poetry collection relates to Ojaide's poetic vision and technique. Okome notes that "new ideologies of life and poetic style are forcing him to capitulate" (Okome:15) and Shija asserts that, Ojaide who had waged a relentless war against dictatorship, social insecurity, corruption, political ineptitude and cultural domination in his earlier works … appears to be losing the war. (Shija: 206). Shija, sharing Okome's view further asserts that "there is certainly no doubt in Okome's observation that Ojaide has shifted in style from a more blunt and forthright attack of social and political system to a more subtle one of introspection" (Shija: 87). Olafioye on the other hand stresses that the shift is from local to universal themes and he writes:

The poet can now take advantage of his circumstance of distance of the periphery of insanity, to celebrate refreshing and rewarding riches of universal life. Thus he welcomes the four winds of the earth into his poetry. He finds needed relief from his usual political humdrum and instead embrace the internationalism of his human experiences (Olafioye: 138).

The claim that Ojaide has shifted from his poetic ideology and style is a misconception because he consistently portrays his predominant social vision, which is socio-economic problems and especially their consequences on the masses. The poetic ideologies which Shija enumerated for instance are the messages that preoccupy the nine different poems titled "Home Songs i-ix" among others. Ojaide in fact raised the issues militating against the well-being of the masses thereby propelling his Marxist ideology to its zenith in this collection more than other collections. Apart from the issue of environment degradation, poverty and its attendant problems of hunger, destitution, disease and death, Ojaide also portrays lack of social amenities such as potable water and light. In "Home Song IV", he blames lack of informal education that parents give to their children through folktales, on lack of electricity. It is also responsible for the "scattered wheezes of dying generators" (118) which pollute the air to the extent that "nobody knows the mood of the sky/ that covers its face with a grey sheet" (118). He reiterates that lack of pipe-borne water has forced the masses to buy "water … in Gerry cans" (118).

The poet has not deviated from his "forth right attack" on the ruling class as Shija asserts either. The language he employ to satirize them in other poems is still evident in *When It No Longer Matters Where You Live*. The use of animal images to satirize the leaders is the attribute of his African indigenous poetic technique, which he adopts to convey his social vision. Ojaide has sustained this technique in all his poetry collections. The assertion that there is a shift in his style can be regarded as an understatement. The description of the leader as "hyena" "crocodile" "vulture" "cock of Abuja" "hawks", and the "butcher of Abuja". "corrupt baron" (75) are some of the images evident in other collections. He describes the presidential villa in "Dateline: Abuja" as "lair" (43) where "human sacrifice" is conducted. He refers to the ruling class as "robbers" that wipe out the shares of those who cannot access the public coffers. He also refers to the corrupt practices of the ruling class as "looting riot" that may transform the people of the nation into destitutes or "homeless within (Its) frontiers" (55). Out of anger he describes Nigeria as "a nation of thieves".

Although Shija thinks that Ojaide "appears to be losing the war" and the "evidence of this is conveyed in the "despondency and docility of masses portrayed" yet he was quick to add that his reading is limited to "the poems analysed in this collection so far". The only poem that reflects the suffering of the masses which he analysed is "Libation" and one can not reach a conclution after reading only a single poem in relation to a particular subject. Undoubtedly, Ojaide has in some of his poems attacked the passivity of the masses. In the "opening song" for instance, he laments that "I am ashamed that impotence caught everyone" (29). In the poem "in dirt and pride" he states that "hardship has smothered the fire brands/ (that) once blazed a liberation trail" (75) and in 'Libation" he attacks his people's complacency in these lines: "…my people still fold their arms and wait/ for reprieve without massing out from cell0"s (40). These attacks on the masses is what Shija refers to as the docility of the masses and "capitalist ideologies" which he insinuates that Ojaide upholds. Attacking the passivity of the masses does not mean that he is upholding bourgeois ideologies but the portraits he lifts are meant to conscientize and reorient mindset of the masses. What Ojaide achieves agrees with Max Horkhiemer's advocacy that "by making the downtrodden man shockingly aware of his despair, the work of art announced freedom which makes them fume" (Selden: 83).

It is pertinent to note that in most of the poems where Ojaide attacks the docility of the masses, he often and consistently conscientizes them. After he attacks the docility of the masses in "opening song" by saying that "I am ashamed that impotence has caught everyone", he again states in the concluding line that "now I sing the wakeful song of the cock" (29) which is meant "to wake the community from stupor". This is by implication, a revolutionary call, which Bertolt Brecht describes as shaking the people "out of their complacent passivity into active engagement" (Selden: 81). In 'Libation" he also declares repeatedly that the fate of the elephant is uncertain as "one (of its) legs(is) in the deeps the other hanging on land". This means that the suffering of the masses is transient since the elephant will die. He also states "in dirt and pride" that his "rage (will) smash the corrupt baron/… (that) shreds every note/ that reinforces a wakening call". These are all indications that Ojaide is not unaware of the harsh realities but he expresses optimism in his ability to conscientize and incite the masses which is only the responsibility of the artist because the "emancipation of the workers is a task of (the) workers themselves" (Critique Sociale, Marh 21st 2009).

Ojaide remains highly optimistic about the overthrow of the ruling class and he expresses such optimism "In Our History" (*The Eagles Vision*). Although he asserts in poem titled "Undercurrent" that "not every step for all its pressure, publish/it presence", yet he optimistically declare that there is "a tribe of servers/waiting for the unknown hour to overturn fate/ and celebrate the inevitable reprieve of change" (44). Ojaide maintains the same lexical term "inevitable" to describe the over-throw of the ruling class, in "Exception" (*Delta Blues and Homesong*). He also expresses an unwavering optimism, despite the diabolic practice that makes the "high stool" to be "daily daubed with blood" (49) in the bid to "arrest the …fall", but he declares that the "fall" is "inevitable". In Ojaide's conscientization of the masses (peasants and proletariat) the use of Marxist ideology and African folkloric genre that have obviously opened wide the gate of liberation of the oppressed and established the Marxist aesthetics in Nigeria.

Works Cited

Bodunde, Charles. "Tanure Ojaide's Poetry and the Delta Landscape: A Study of *Delta Blues and Home Songs*" Onookome Okome (ed.) *Writing the Homeland: The Poetry and Politics of Tanure Ojaide*. Bayreuth University Press, 2002.

Bressler, Charles. *An Introduction to Theory and Practices*. New Jessey: Prentice-Hall Inc. 1999.

Doble, Ann. *Theory into Practice*. Canada: Thompson Learning Inc. 2002. http://libcon.prg/liberty/basic: principles – Marxism – Critique-Sociale.

Lynn, Stephen. *Text and Contents: Writing About Literature with Critical Theory* South Califonia: Addison-Wesley, Educational Publishers Inc. 2001.

Ojaide, Tanure and Obi, Joseph. *Culture, Society and Politics in Modern African Poetry,* Carolina Durilam NC Carolina Academy Press 1996.

Ojaide, Tanure. *Delta Blues and Homesongs*. Ibadan: Karft Books Ltd, 1997.

_____ *The Eagle's Vision*, Detroit: Lotus Press, 1987.

_____ *The Endless Songs*. Lagos: Malthouse: 1989.

_____ *When It No Longer Matters Where You Live,* Calabar: Calabar University Press, 1998.

Okome, Onookome. (ed.) *Writing the Homeland: The Poetry and Politics of Tanure Ojaide.* Bayrenth: Bayreuth University Press, 2002. p.15.

Olafioye, Taiwo. *The Poetry of Tanure Ojaide: A Critical Appraisal* Lagos: Malthouse Press 2000.

Olaoluwa, Sanayan S. "Where Do We Go from Here? Niger-Delta Crumbling Urbanspacepe and Migration in Tanure Ojaide's *When it No Longer Matters Where You Live*. www.olaoluwasananya2007@yahoo.com.

Selden, Raman and Peter Windowson. *Contemporary Literature Theory*. Britain: Kentucky University Press. 1993.

Shija, Terhemba. *Post-Coloniality and the Poetry of Tanure Ojaide*. Makurdi: Aboki Publications. 2006.

Identification through Trauma:
A Psychoanalytical Interpretation of Five Poems in Ojaide's *Songs of Myself*

Linda Jummai Mustafa

Introduction

Tanure Ojaide for more than five decades has undoubtedly talked on environmental concerns of the Niger Delta especially as it relates to oil exploration and the adverse effects of environmental degradation, the pilfering of the Delta people's resources without compensation, poverty, political hegemony by the Nigerian government that abandons the people of the Delta despite the sacrificial release of their lands for oil exploration. Because of these and many more activities that brings a further restructuring of the Niger Delta, there has been a lot of academic researches carried out on Ojaide's poetry and novels which are mainly focused on environmental issues. Speaking on his art, Enajite Ojaruega (2014) explicitly notes Ojaide's tendencies, here stated:

… Much of Ojaide's poetry consistently dwells on the paradox of an oil wealth that is a blessing turned doom, a curse rather than a source of joy for his people and region. Strong strains of lamentation and nostalgic evocation for what was once an idyllic environment, but now greatly damaged, are also found in his poetry. (93)

Similarly, Tayo Olafioye (2000) believes that "Tanure Ojaide's poetry present multi-layered themes, wrought in contemporary reality". (46). He goes on to say that the themes of Ojaide's poems include amongst many others the themes of historical realities, political images, grandmother persona's, rural dexterity, the degradation of the lands of the Niger-Delta and love. Ojaide is therefore a man so enveloped by love of his community that he carries part of the Delta along with him wherever he goes. Perhaps, Ojaide's connectedness to the Delta makes him write unrelentingly about his people despite his exposure to the western world. The Delta is always with him as he attests in the following: "My roots thus run deep into the delta area…Home remains for me the Delta, where I continue to anchor myself" (World Literature Today 15 Winter 1994).

It is therefore not surprising that yet again, Ojaide's *Songs of Myself: Quartet* celebrates the life of an old man who intimates the youths on how to behave in an "ecological and environmental damaged Niger Delta" (Ojaide 6). Although, several reviews and analysis of this book of poems have been made through the postcolonial theory and other literary theories to critique environmental degradation; however, for this study, the theoretical meaning of trauma will be used to analyse Ojaide's *Songs of Myself* to decipher the psychic determinants of the persona in this work. In the use of psychoanalysis to understudy Ojaide's *Songs of Myself*, this study shall uncover how the persona in the work, overcomes a haunted past to locate his unique identity in order to be a figure reckoned with in his society. Despite his bad experiences, his exile, his loneliness, his apprehension and his resolve to stay alive at all cost, the persona in *Songs of Myself* evolved and gained a modified reputable self.

Literature Review

In their analysis of Ojaide's poetry, both Jide Balogun (2006, 78) and Ayinde Abdullahi (2011) see his writings "as a vehicle for political mediation and social control" (78). Hence, Ayinde explains further that Ojaide's sensibility to the thievery of a people's resources without care for their sustainability constitutes the greater part of the deplorable state of the Delta as stated in the following: "Corruption has become one of the major antinomies that create a deepening crisis of kleptocracy; it engenders a scandalous wealth among the ruling class with growing poverty, misery and degradation among the masses" (Ayinde 103).

Uzoechi Nwagbara (2008) describes the poet as using "literature for environmentalist purposes" as "he places premium on the biotic community—its sustainability and preservation" (18). Ojaide also restlessly exposes the violations of the people's economic right, particularly the economic exploitation of the minority Niger Delta region of the country. He therefore, feels that as a poet, he is duty bound to use "craft to explore marginalization and dehumanization" (Ma'at, 2005, 221). Similarly, Orabueze (2008,165) expresses that Ojaide beams his poetic searchlight on the dispossession of the cultural heritage of the people. More significantly, Ojaide places premium on the biotic community - its sustainability and preservation. This literary pattern is in congruence with "aesthetics of the earth" (Glissant 149).

Ojaruega has also assessed Ojaide's use of orature in his poetry. She writes that: "...it is apparent that Ojaide uses orature to establish not only a cultural identity for his work but also organize style and form to effectively express his themes. In doing so, the poet also gives the present generation and readers an idea of their traditional heritage and how it can be used to express current and enduring thoughts and feelings. Within Ojaide's poetry, contemporary issues are sometimes reconstructed through similar episodes and events found in past Urhobo traditional oral history and folkloric heritage" ("The Place" 143). And again, Enajite Ojaruega assesses the environmental activism of Tanure Ojaide's poetry and concludes that:

…Much of Ojaide's poetry consistently dwells on the paradox of an oil wealth that is a blessing turned doom, a curse rather than a source of joy for his people and region. Strong strains of lamentation and nostalgic evocation for what was once an idyllic environment, but now greatly damaged, are also found in his poetry ("The Place"138-139).

Finally, the trio of Dike Okoro (2007, 1), Aderemi Bamikunle (1991, 81) and C.G. Darah (2009) see Ojaide's poetry as resistance poetry. They all believe that Ojaide's consistent search to locate his people's identity takes him through pre-colonial ancestral history, colonialism and the current multinational insensitivity. Darah's point of view best summarizes the conception of the aforementioned academics views on Ojaide's use of poetry as mean of resistance from the following excepts:

The poetry of Tanure Ojaide … fits into the tradition of outrage against political injustice, exploitation and environmental disasters. On the basis of sheer output, Ojaide is the most prolific in the Niger delta region. From his titles, one can discern an abiding concern with the fate of the Niger delta people… Many of the poems in these collections are verbal missiles directed at political despots whose rule has brought misery and distress to the region. (12)

The Psychoanalytic Theory of Trauma

Since Freud's postulation of psychoanalysis in the early 1930s, there has been varied postulations of the concept. For some scholars, psychoanalysis is a school of psychology, which emphasizes psychic determinism and dynamics. As a school of psychology, it also emphasizes the importance of childhood experiences in molding one's adult personality and behaviour. Secondly, other psychoanalysts see psychoanalysis as a specialised method for investigating the unconscious mental activities and thirdly, psychoanalysis is a therapeutic method for the investigation and treatment of mental disorders, especially the neurotic disorders. For this paper, the emphasis on psychic determinants through the understanding of the trauma theory, will feature prominently in the analysis of the persona in Ojaide's work.

For years now, flash backs and nightmares are considered the aftermath of a victim's encounter with a distressing past event that may be difficult to forget.

The unforgettable worrying of the past can take a huge toll on an individual's mental and physical health hence culminating to a psychiatric case. This situation, is what has resulted to advance study of the theory of trauma, which can be seen as the effects that are imprinted on a person's psyche after having undergone an intense emotional experience that manifests as recurring dreams or nightmares, and which makes it difficult for the individual to move on. Trauma is also described as an experience that a person undergoes which devastates them as a result of horrific events, such that they may have uninvited recurring images (Caruth, 1996). These recurring nightmares and hallucinations that disturb an individual from time to time are considered manifestations of trauma. Trauma can prevent an individual from moving on in life; it disrupts all or any normalcy and causes much upheaval.

The work of Cathy Caruth, who is one of the central figures in fostering the development of cultural theory in the early 1990s, suggested that traumatic events can overwhelm the psychic defenses and normal processes of registering memory traces (Caruth, 1991b, 417). In other words, trauma is seared directly into the psyche; "almost like a piece of shrapnel, and is not subject to the distortions of subjective memory". (Caruth, 1991a, 3). Yet it is precisely because of this unusual memory registration, that what may be most traumatic is that which does not appear in conscious memory. Therefore, Caruth (1996a, 91-92) says: "Traumatic experience is a paradox; that the most direct seeing of a violent event may occur as an absolute inability to know it." In her book titled *Unclaimed Experience: Trauma, Narrative, and History*, Caruth acknowledged Sigmund Freud's definition of trauma as a wound that is inflicted upon the body here presented:

The wound of the mind- the breach in the mind's experience of time, self and the world is not, like the wound of the body, a simple and healable event, but rather an event that…is experienced too soon, too unexpectedly, to be fully known and is therefore not available to consciousness until it imposes itself again, repeatedly, in the nightmares and repetitive actions of the survivor. (qtd in Caruth 4)

And she then provides the general definition of trauma as: "The response to an unexpected or

overwhelming violent event or events that are not fully grasped as they occur, but return later in repeated flashbacks, nightmares, and other repetitive phenomena." (91).

According to Roger Luckhurst (2008, 2), gender, sexual or racial violence, individual identities as well as national collective memories are indirectly shaped by trauma. In fact, the memory worth remembering is that of trauma. (Antze and Lambek, 1996, p. xii). Dominick LaCapara (2001, 21) comments that trauma could be a potential threat to identification because trauma can "confuse self and the other" thus collapsing all distinctions. Again, Caruth (1996a) studied Freud's *Beyond the Pleasure Principle* and notes that Freud believes "that psychological trauma does not occur in strict correspondence to the body's experience of a life threat, that is, through the wounding of the body" (60). To Caruth, traumatic experiences often reoccur in dreams which stimulates repressed memories and this may cause a person to be "fixated to his/her trauma." Since traumatic experiences may reoccur in dreams, then what causes this recurrence? Caruth answers this question by saying:

What causes, trauma, then, is a shock that appears to work very much like a bodily threat but is in fact a break in the mind's experience of time… We may, I think, tentatively venture to regard the common traumatic neurosis as a consequence of an extensive breach being made in the protective shield against stimuli… And we still attribute importance to the element of fright. It is caused by lack of any preparedness for anxiety. (1996a, 62)

Caruth goes on to explain that this breach in the mind is what Freud suggest is the lack of preparedness to take in a stimulus that comes too quickly.

Although, traumatic events are best forgotten than relived, most authors however feel the need to transmit, the pain suffered by individuals, communities or sometimes themselves through their art, Caruth's (1996a) observation here stated explains this need to transmit pain: "Trauma seems to be much more than a pathology, or the simple illness of a wounded psyche: it is always the story of a wound that cries out, that addresses us in the attempt to tell us of a reality or truth that is not otherwise available." (4).

Moreover, Judith Lewis Herman (1992) sees trauma as a healing process. To her, rather than avoiding traumatic experiences, one must incorporate trauma into everyday life and therefore says: "The goal of recounting the trauma story is integration, not exorcism." (181). This work agrees with Herman in incorporating trauma in everyday life. Now more than ever, people are experiencing tragic happenings that were once conceived to be mere stories. If one is empowered with the ability to overcome traumatic happenings in their daily life, then it is likely that severe repression (hysteria) or suicidal attempts shall greatly be reduced or totally be eradicated. Thus, studying Ojaide's *Songs of Myself* would enable this research an academic view of the identity of the persona via his traumatic experiences.

Identity and Trauma in *Songs of Myself*

The poem "Without these memories" talks about the numerous flashbacks the persona has about landscapes, the beauty of life, love, music and sufferings. The persona is filled with the need to recount his pain in order to locate his healing. Like Herman (1992, 181) suggests, this paper believes that the persona integrates his past pain to establish an unshakable self:

Without the past spectacle of beauties and scarecrows

Without landmarks standing behind the current station

Without voices echoing from long ago to distract from

Loud silences threatening to benumb primed ears

How would I appreciate today's vibrant music or give

Timaya a graceful nod in my crammed solitary room?

("Without these memories" 33)

In his emotional connection to the past, the persona traces his identity through his carefully guarded memories. As he reminiscence on the barriers that almost mar his identity, he celebrates his present status of overcoming poverty and dejection:

Without these memories charging in and out

Covering and opening up old-time wealth

What poverty would be afflicting me today!

Without the retinue stampeding for recognition

What loneliness would accompany me all year

To destinations of hope set out without a roadmap

("Without these memories" 34)

By implication, the persona's pain becomes the base and strength of his identification. Despite lacking love, wandering the cities and a forced state of celibacy, the poet frightening past which is locked away in his memories is however consciously retrieved for the building up of an unbreakable personality which is now more likable and presentable as compared to his past traumatic personality.

According to Freud (1915), The unconscious mind acts as a repository, a "cauldron" of primitive wishes and impulses kept at bay and mediated by the preconscious area. This situation, may have moved Ojaide to write the poem "What I remember". In the very beginning of the poem, Ojaide re-echo's Freud's stance of the mind being kept at bay: "What I remember I have kept safe…" (35). Here, the persona situates himself in his beautiful abode with a deliberate urge to remember the bloom of the flowers and his love. Soaked in the euphoria of treasured memories, the poet is able to overcome the trauma of a riotous and unstable present with the knowledge that he is able to withstand being brought down by the pains he currently experience:

… When in bloom in an auspicious season

That make me forget the bruises of today's briars.

My love has not lost the luster of old

Because ageless in her prime I caught her;

My love has remained constant all the years

Because of everlasting moment of fulfillment

… I sing of the remembrance of things past,

Things that festoon today with smiles;

I sing the erasure of darkness and smudges

In the sun that rests perpetually on a calm face.

("What I remember" 35-36)

Caruth (1996, 60), notes that traumatic experiences often reoccur in dreams which stimulates repressed memories and this may cause a person to be "fixated to his/her trauma." The poet speaks of a persona who is worried about his travails in a dream state and he wishes to avoid being fixated on his present traumatic experience. The poet then stimulates his subconscious to bring to the fore wonderful memories of the past which he uses to douse thoughts of a gloomy future. He emphatically explains what he remembers of love that gives him much satisfaction in the present as observed in the following:

What I remember of love is stored

With fragrance in a garden of blooming bougainvillea;

The passionate compliments a harvest of reminiscences

That crowd the timescape with contentment. ("What I remember" 35)

From remembering his love, friendship, cordial communal relationship and a peaceful life lived in the past, the poet cannot but situates his troubled roots to his nurtured identity of restfulness, joy and contentment even in the midst of an uncertain future:

I need no aquamarine to soak the timeless tokens,

Need not secure a ring of loyalty in a bank safe;

…What I transfer from one residence to another

Glows with waxing warmth of earth colors;

…The token of friendship remains without rust

Even if an iron band meant to fuel our lust; ("What I remember" 34-35)

In Ojaide's "Self-defense" the disabuse conception of a supposedly "lazy man" seems to bring out an angry remembrance of a biased people. It may be coincidental that Ojaide in his forward for *Songs of Myself* express that "This collection…deals with self-examination and the minstrel's alter-ego as a way of attempting to know himself" (6). This is exactly this paper's objective as we also find a persona in "self-defense", examining himself to get over his trauma as well as the negative name tag he has been given by members of his community. This apparent misconception of the persona as a "loafer" by his community affects his independent identity and he his angry as he recalls all his heroic deeds for his community:

They say I am the loafer, the stay-at-home one

And everybody smacks me with terrible insults!

When the warrior chief's home caught fire in his absence

I spotted it and alerted folks to stop the savage blaze;

When the wealthy farmer's mother took ill and collapsed

I, the reviled loafer, the stay-at-home one, revived her.

("Self-defense" 91)

Ojaide's central preoccupation in this poem is the location of a buried traumatic past of a man who never fails to come to the rescue of distress persons. Instead of extoling his heroic deeds and personal sacrifice, he is ridiculed by the entire members of his community. Because the society labels him a "stay-at home", no good for nothing man, his confident personality is ruffled and he is shaken by their action of ingratitude:

They say I haven't the bile it takes in the liver

To kill a snake not to talk of catching a snakefish,

They say I am like rock salt used in preparing dishes

And would melt and so cannot fish or farm in the rain

But I am sent on errands, the town-crier of every season.

I composed the chant that makes leopards of warriors;

In days of Biafra I spotted camouflaged saboteurs

Before military intelligence recovered from rape orgies. ("Self-defense" 91)

The poet expresses his bitterness at not being recognised by his people for his numerous inspiring songs and his tenacious will to serve his people. He is mocked by the people he puts his life down to defend and the credit for composing such inspiring songs is allotted to other performers because he is poor and unemployed. In the following lines readers can perceive his agony: "of course our performers always take the credit for them/as those like me everywhere dispossessed and silenced" (91). The trauma of not being recognised as the composer of inspiring chants that moves warriors to victory, further deteriorates his identification with his community. Through his lamentation, this research observe that the persona is confused. He is divided on whether to do more for his community and still be called a loafer, or regain confidence in himself and damn the insults pelted on him. In his "self defence", as the poem is so titled, the persona's rants actually propel him towards establishing a confident independent identity which does not rob him off his happiness.

The poem "Apprehension" can be said to conjure up a sense of mystery, worry, uncertainty, chaos and an infinite fear of the unknown. In this poem, the mention of the "Tortoise", "Aridon", "the indestructible bronze of Benin, fire spitting fighter", "cobra" and "antelope" all denotes a representation of the African way of life shackled in spirituality and mysticism. Ojaide directs the attention of readers to the mystic identity of the persona, especially drawing readers' imagination to a character that is entrenched in the traditional values/mystery of his people:

The tortoise taunts the tar doll with insults

The tar doll apprehends the talker with silence

O Aridon, take away the brassy rattle from me

But leave me the indestructible bronze of Benin

The fire-spitting fighter's consumed by his flames

Take away the smoke and leave me unstoppable fire

I muffle my voice in the city of prattlers and gossips

("Apprehension" 154)

The persona does not get scars of shame from idle insults and gossips, instead he builds his self-confidence by imploring the gods to come to his aids.

According to Hooks (1992, 172) one can easily bear a traumatic past by deliberately going back to the time, place and location of a frightening event which has long been forgotten. Ojaide may have had Hooks postulation in mind when he makes his persona to go back in time to locate what ails him so much that images of animals fill his thoughts. The presentation of animals such as hyenas and falcons stimulates the persona's vision of strength, craftiness, swiftness and resilience, all characteristics of a confident, independent and diligent identity. The persona heals from his past mistake by taking solace in the fact that he is not the first to have committed several crimes and the world particularly is filled with people who have committed other similarly grievous crimes. The reconciliation he makes with his inner self, brings him an outward peace, hence the persona's unusually unabashed confidence in the man he has become:

I throw my phallus to the hyenas to be a new man

Since wife-beaters justify savagery with body parts

I sire a clan of adorable children without lovemaking

I know the whole world without leaving my room

The antelope is not a drum but none without its death

Martyr the antelope to transmit codes in the land of spirits

The cobra does not bite or swell to deter molestation

But who's so brave he dares catch it with bare hands?

("Apprehension" 154)

The portrayal of the picture of a man who may be remorseful of disregarding the norms and values of the land, especially directs this paper's attention to the persona's guilt in having children without a stable lover or wife. He is knowledgeable in all the wiles of the world from his room and with his knowledge of evil practices done all over the world, he empowers himself with an identity that traumatizes his being as well as others. The poet asks in wonderment "…who's so brave he dares catch it [a snake] with bare hands?"(154), directing readers' attention to the fact that a man without knowing his worth or strength cannot dare catch a snake with his bare hands. Therefore, in order to identify with his community, Ojaide's persona resolves to master his memories, traumas, pains and joys such that his identity is discernable by the community and even himself: "Aridon, let my eloquence not come through a loud mouth/Let my entire body not only speak for but lead me" ("Apprehension" 154)

Finally, another poem that portray the picture of trauma and identity formation is the poem "Let them die for Arsenal". Here Ojaide vehemently expresses his disgust at how African communities and particularly most Nigerian communities, are incapacitated when gruesome crimes are committed. The "I don't care" nature of Nigerians towards corruption and other grievous crimes, especially draws readers' attention to a deteriorating nation in all the spheres of life as can be deduced from the following except of the poem "Let them die for Arsenal":

…Those who do nothing seeing their property carted away

Those who watch their mothers, wives, and daughters raped

Those who pay phantom light bills for blackouts months

Those whose reps steal their share of the national wealth

Those who abandon their children in war to save themselves

("Let them die for Arsenal" 165)

From the preceding except, it is obvious that many Nigerians are not confident enough to put a stop to tyrannical happenings around them. For many, their identities are shrouded in trauma hence their incapacity to respond to dire situation. In this poem, the poet is extremely aghast at the peoples' will not to react when they are being molested, cheated, abused and uncared for. Indeed, this kind of nonchalant behaviour, shocks the poet and he is forced to lament the careless disregard of life by members of a society and a nation.

Furthermore, the poet situates his memory of the lackadaisical character of community members whose inaction has caused untold pains, hardship and even death. Unlike the numerous football fans worldwide, Nigerians have lost an identity of communal togetherness which is the sole factor, initiating irresponsibility. A typical Nigerian man is not bold enough to speak out his mind towards the ills being committed in his domain. To fight for his rights becomes a tough battle as he is not ready to die for what he believes in. His trauma at having lost his uniqueness, his individuality, his independence and right of life therefore makes him accept whatever evil done to himself and his community:

Let them die for Arsenal

Those who raise not arms against brutish police and soldiers

Those who choose to accept kola rather than the simple truth

Those who "hammer" rather than live honest hard work

Those who stop not after perilous potholes to plant a red flag

Those who refuse to be eyes of the blind and feet of the crippled

Those who sell body parts to build mansions they won't live in

    ("Let them die for Arsenal" 165)

Ojaide continues his lamentation of a dying life style of togetherness by citing others that have overcome humiliation through acts of patriotism in supporting a football team to the letter: "…die for Arsenal, die for all the Europa clubs/And let the strong breed here live on/Die for Asernal and rid the land of contagion/Die for Arsenal and rid the land of psychos and suicides" (165). Moreover, Ojaide equally acknowledges the pain of dying unpleasantly from avoidable situations. He equally talks down on peoples' conscious effort to die without a definite cause which distorts the need to live a life well spent. Such deaths from the likes of "Holy Ghost fire", "witchcraft", "poisonous snakebite", "motor crash", "massive heart attack" (166) and other kinds of similarly avoidable deaths, are situations which the poet feels demean the identity of a person because a person expecting to die in such ways has not in any way built an indisputable identity. He (Ojaide) therefore elicit readers' responsibility towards living a life full of hope and desires rather than crouching in the abyss of uncertainties and un-identity.

The poet goes on to admonish that a person can overcome trauma by having a definite dream, vision and desire. Even though trauma may try to dent a person's identity, when that person is faced with a choice to live or die, he most definitely wants to live and in living there must be a cause that he lives for as stated thus:

You don't die for many causes

You don't die for Arsenal and still die for Nigeria

You die only for one cause

You don't die for Arsenal and still bring back our stolen children

There is only one death

Die for Arsenal and you are gone as a person (166)

According to Abraham Maslow (1970 & 1987), once safety and physiological needs are met, higher, more typically "human" needs come to the foreground. This basic social or affiliation motive, drives people to seek contact with others and to build satisfying relations with them. This perhaps may be the message Ojaide wants to pass on to Nigerians. In order to identify with one's community or nation, a person has to commit himself/herself to a cause that promotes love and understanding: "You have only one life/ throw it away for Arsenal and desecrate your homeland" (166). In fact, a Nigerian should be so passionate that any breech of peace may culminate to his earnest will to restore peace, and this resolve could cause him his life which he should be willing to do, to show his love for his people and his nation. In "Let them die for Arsenal", Maslow's concept of psychological and safety needs, artfully explain why Ojaide berates the lack of will to live and defend one's rights. To Ojaide's keen observation, a lot of Nigerians are busy pursuing ventures that don't promote love, sense of belonging and the development of their society. This is why many Nigerians look the other way when gruesome crimes are committed against them. So the reaction of Nigerians to die like "fools", as "homeless relatives", "stray rabid dog" (166-167) can be avoidable only if Nigerians can stand and defend their will to live.

Conclusion

This paper has looked at how the experience of trauma locates the identity of a person in order to transform his life in a positive or negative way depending on the person's disposition to trauma. In this paper, we find that despite all the sufferings of the persona in the poems studied, Ojaide artfully links the crisis of traumatized persons to self-development and acceptance of life trials. For instance, in the poem "Let them die for Arsenal", Ojaide glaringly express boldly his quest to see a patriotic Nigerian who will put first the survival of the nation rather than his prosperity. In wanting to be gratified, a person wants to be esteemed by the people around him, hence the lamentation of his disvalued input to the community by the persona in "Self-defense". And in the poems "Without these memories", "Apprehension" and "What I remember" there is the observation of the formation of strong personalities who identify with their communities even as they suffer numerous trials. These personalities question their achievements in relation to their self-development and they become gratified by the fact that they have touched one life or the other as they struggle to become who they want to be.

Works Cited

Antze, Paul. & Michael, Lambek, editors. *Tense Past: Cultural Essays in Trauma and Memory*, 1996.

Ayinde, Abdullahi Kadir. "Festus Iyayi's The Contracts as a Replica of the Nigerian Society."

Journal of the Nigeria English Studies Association (JNESA), vol. 14. No. 2, Sept. 2011,

pp.103-111.

Balogun, Jide. "The Poet as a Social Crusader: Tanure Ojaide and the Poetry of Intervention."

Journal of Humanities, vol. 20, 2006, pp. 78-

88.<https://www.ajol.info/index.php/jh/article/view/153375/142967>. Accessed 15 March 2018.

Bamikunle, Aderemi. "Literature as a Historical Process: A Study of Ojaide's Labyrinths of the Delta". Chidi Ikonne, et al. editors. *African Literature and African Historical Experiences*, HEB, 1999.

Caruth, Cathy. *Unclaimed experience: Trauma, narrative, and history.* The John Hopkins

University Press, 1996a.

—-"Introduction to Psychoanalysis, Trauma and Culture I". *American Imago*, vol. 48, no. 1,

1991a, p. 3.

—-"Introduction to Psychoanalysis, Trauma and Culture II". *American Imago*, vol. 48, no.4, 1991b, pp. 417.

Glissant, Edouard. *Poetics of Relation.* Translated by Betsy Wing. Uni. of Michigan Press, 1999.

Herman, Judith. *Trauma and Recovery.* Basic Books, 1992.

Hooks, Bell. *Black Looks: Race and Representation.* South End Press, 1992.

Dara, G.G. "Revolutionary Pressures in Niger Delta Literatures". *Guardian*, 28, June 2009, pp. 10-12.

Lacapra, D. "Acting-out and Working Through Trauma." Interviewed by A. Goldberg [in person] Cornell University. June 9 1998.

Ma'at Sharifa Saa Atma. "In Search of a New Self". In Makward, Edris, et al. editors. *North*

South Linkages and Connections in Continental and Diaspora African Literatures.

African Literature Association Annual Series, vol. 12, 2005, pp. 220-238.

Maslow, Abraham. Hierarchy of Needs. https://web.archive.org/web20100211014419/

https://Honolulu.hawaii.edu/intranet/committees/FacDevCom/guidebk/teachtip/maslow.htm.

Accessed 19 March 2018.

—- *Motivation and Personality.* 2nd ed., Harper & Row, 1970.

—- Motivation and Personality. 3rd ed., revised by R. Frager, J. Fadima, et al. Harper & Row,1987.

Okoro, Dike. http://www.african.com/articles/227/1/ojaide-sings-th-tale- . Accessed 20

April 2018.

Ojaide, Tanure. *Songs of Myself: Quartet,* Kraft Books, 2015.

Ojaruega, Enajite E. "Urhobo Literature in English: A Survey". Aridon: The Journal of Urhobo

Studies 1, 2014, pp. 87–102.

—- "The Place of Urhobo Folklore in Tanure Ojaide's Poetry." Tydskrif vir Letterkunde, Vol. 52.2, 2015, pp.138-158. <https://www.scielo.org.za/pdf/tvl/v52n2/10.pdf>. Accessed 10 April 2018.

Orhero, Mathias I. "Urhobo Folklore and Udje Aesthetics in Tanure Ojaide's *In the House of*

Words and Songs of Myself."CLCWeb*: Comparative Literature and Culture*, Vol.19. No 2, 2017.https://doi.org/10.7771/1481-4374.3014. Accessed 11 April 2018.

World Literature Today. Vol. 15 Winter, 1994.

A Socio-stylistic appraisal of selected poems in Tanure Ojaide's The Eagle's Vision

Moshood Zakariyah & Mariam Titilope Gobir

Introduction

Poetry is an important literary genre whose style is highly distinctive from the other literary genres. Apart from the structural and linguistic characteristics of poetry which clearly mark its distinctiveness, individual poets have specific styles of writing that are peculiar to them. Tanure Ojaide's poetry among his other works with which he has contributed to African literature is unique as evident in his linguistic choices and themes. His style of writing always portrays his ideology on literature as a cultural production. His linguistic deployment does not only convey his artistic creativity as an African writer but also reflect his disposition towards socio-economic, political and environmental marginalisation and religious intolerance. These and a host of others are preponderant in his works.

It is generally believed that the identification of the marked linguistic features of a given text or a series of texts, either spoken or written, literary or non-literary, and the description of the identified linguistic features in relation to their significances in the text with the aim of emphasising linguistic variations are the essentials of stylistics. Contemporary writers deviate from the linguistic norms in their writing styles to reflect their innermost thoughts and visions. In most cases, deviations occur to achieve communication of authorial intentions, especially to the potential audience. At times, these deviations are inevitable as they reflect the ethnic and socio-political background of writers. The examination of selected poems from Tanure Ojaide's collection—*The Eagle's Vision* from a socio-stylistic perspective is the focus of this study. The poet's deployment of the linguistic elements and the contributions of the linguistic choices to the textual interpretation are also examined to demystify the myth behind the poetic choices.

Style, Stylistics and Poetry

Just like man and his varying preference of colours, style as a concept has over the years been garbed in robes of different opinions and definition. There has been –particularly- amongst linguist, a dissention as to what style really is, and a further dissention as to how it can be defined wholesomely, in a single sentence. Paul Simpson defined stylistics as "a method of textual interpretation in which primacy of place is assigned to language" (2). This definition by

Simpson viewed style as the ability to use language with adequate aesthetics in diverse contexts. A more distinct view is taken by Albert Sydney Hornby, to him; style is the "manner of writing that is the characteristics of a particular writer, historical period or type of literature" (10). This view was corroborated by Ronald Carter and Enkvist, Spencer and Gregory. To Carter, style was perceived as "distinctive and identifiable form in an artistic medium". Style in this sense is thus viewed from the perspective of the different traits and entails of individual writer, periods and literary genres.

Stylistics on the other hand is the analytical study of style. It is a branch of linguistics that is concerned with the presence, usage, and function of style of language users. Other than this, the term stylistics connotes various things to various scholars. To some scholars, Stylistics is an objective and scientific study of language usage in a text which seeks to mediate between linguistics and literary criticism. Amongst the scholars with this view of stylistics is Henrry Widdowson who opined that "stylistics is linguistic analysis of text—the combination of both literature as text and literature as discourse is what stylistics does" (23). From Widdowson's definition of Stylistics we can infer that Stylistics studies the usage of language in a text through an empirical rather than an impressionistic approach. In the same vein, Geoffrey Leech and Micky Short corroborated Widdowson's view on Stylistics. To them, Stylistics is "the linguistic approach to literature explaining the relation between language and artistic function, with motivating questions such as why, how and what" (58). This opinion of Leech and Short seems to encapsulate the practicality of Stylistics as discipline of text analysis through linguistic tools.

Stylistics, still to other scholars, is viewed as a sub-discipline of Linguistics that is concerned with the systematic analysis of style in language use and how this can vary according to factors such as genre, context, historical period, and author. Amongst the scholars holding this view of Stylistics are Enkvist, Spencer and Gregory. To them Stylistics borrows from the models, techniques and methodologies of linguistics to actualise its analysis of text. This invariably ascertains its sub-linguistic nature as it relies and depends on it to thrive. Hence what is safe to assert is that style is a key compartment of stylistics as stylistics is the vehicle through which the concept of style in the academia thrives.

Stylistics applies linguistics to literature in the hope of arriving at analyses which are more broadly based, rigorous, and objective. It is a field of study that takes into account the various intricacies of style in texts irrespective of its literary or none literary nature. As a branch of linguistics, stylistics commonly attempts to analyse and describe the workings of texts which have already been selected as noteworthy on other grounds. Here, the analysis can appear objective, detailed and technical. One of the reasons behind the popularity of stylistics is its warmness and reception towards other field; literature particularly. One could be inquisitive as to: *why employ stylistics in doing poetry?* An overt response to this question is that: *form is important to poetry, and stylistics has the largest tools of analytical weapons.* Therefore, stylistics is a linguistic approach that accounts for the intricacies of poems, and explicates the functions and implications of these intricacies.

Theoretical Considerations

The theoretical basis for this study constitutes a blend of sociolinguistic and stylistic theories. The sociolinguistic approach adopted for the study is the Cultural Identity Theory while the stylistic theory is Linguistic Pluralism. Culture denotes the way of life of a group of people, it varies across speech communities and social groups. Cultural identity refers to people's possession of sense of belonging to a group. It is the extent to which one is a representative of a given culture morally, linguistically, psychologically and sociologically. It reflects common historical experiences and shared cultural codes which give a group of people a feeling of oneness, single entity, a stable, unchanging, continuing frame of reference and meaning. People's judgments about whether they or others belong to a cultural group can be influenced by physical appearance, ancestral origin or personal behaviour. Historical event(s), political conditions, situation of interaction and public discourse, also affect people's cultural identity. Cultural identity is not static as it constantly evolves over time. It covers the entire life span of human beings and changes every moment based on social context. Cultural identity is constantly shifting the understanding of one's identity in relation to others.

Cultural Identity theory suggests a relationship between inter-cultural competence and cultural identity. The theory deals with the study into how individuals use communicative processes to construct and negotiate their cultural group identities and relationships in particular contexts. The theory explicates that culture is one of the many identities expressed in communication encounters. Cultural identity is reflected through social comparison. Speakers compare the position of their own groups to those of other groups. An individual's message during interaction will contain multiple cultural identities such as nationalist, racist, ethnic, class related, sex, gender based, political and religious.

Collier and Thomas described seven properties of cultural identity. These properties refer to the manners in which members of a group communicate their identity. The first is Avowal and Ascription, which describes how cultural identities are produced and the ways in which these identities are communicated. One concept juxtaposes the other. Avowal is the articulation or expression of individual views about group identity. It is the presentation of oneself to another person. Ascription reflects other people's perception of an individual which does not belong to their group. It is how one refers to others which is often stereotypical. Avowed qualities versus ascribe qualities leads to conflicts which resolutions depend on the status position of group members.

Second is the modes of expression, which is indicated with the use of core symbols such as names, labels and norms that a cultural community share and follow to show that they belong to a group, a demonstration of shared identity. Collier discovered that there were similarities in cultural norms of each ethnic group and there are within group differences regarding gender and nature of relationship. The next is the three components of cultural identity— individual, relational and communal. The first, individual, refers to how an individual interprets his cultural identity based on his experiences; relational refers to how individuals interact with one another and communal identity is the use of communication in the creation, affirmation and negotiation of shared identity. The fourth is the enduring and changing aspects of cultural identity. The cultural identity changes due to several factors which are social, political, economic and contextual. The affective, cognitive and behavioral aspects of cultural identity follows. This refers to emotions fully attached to cultural identity situations.

The content and relationship level is the sixth. This refers to the interaction between two or more individuals. Here, the participants of the conversation interpret the choice and meanings of the words based on their experiences. The interactions also show the relational level based on how a person delivers the message. The last of the principles is prominence which refers to how much a person's cultural identity stands out and attracts attention. This is influenced by the extent of similarity or difference between two individuals. The intensity differs depending on context, situation topic and relationship.

Michael Hecht, Mary Collier, and Sidney Ribeau acknowledged the need for more direct examination of identity negotiation processes: "If identities are negotiated in everyday conversation and if identity negotiation is a process, then we need much more information about the negotiation process itself" (173). Both Collier and Jackson accepted this challenge and constructed their own theories of identity negotiation. Collier offered the cultural identity negotiation theory, which had evolved from the cultural identity theory .Among the critics of the cultural theory of identity was Yulia Zeytseva who claimed that:

CTI is an appealing communication theory with a considerable heuristic power. It goes beyond simply providing a list of loosely integrated theoretical propositions, which some theories do, and attempts to construct a coherent framework for communication analysis of multiple and shifting postmodern "saturated" identities (28).

Also, Peter Burke and Jan Stets posited that cultural theory of identity presents a way of bringing together under one theoretical roof, analyses of personal identities, relational roles, and group identifications, which before presented a gap in identity theorizing (224).

The pluralists' perspective on stylistic study is tagged dualism and monism. The two concepts are major approaches to the study of stylistics which refer to 'content' and 'form'. Form is the essential organisational structure or formal features of a text. The content on the other hand, is the subject matter, more expressively, what Michael Halliday (153) referred to as the Ideational Structure of a text. Analysing the form of a text demands the identification of grammatical parallels and assemblage of all the grammatical structures that are similar and opposite to compare and see if there are relationships between them in order to account for the aesthetic qualities and value of the language. Pluralists disagree with the functions of language and how language functions are manifested in literary language.

According to the pluralist, language performs a number of different functions and any piece of language is likely to be the result of choices made on different functional levels. The pluralists are interested in how choices of language are interrelated to one another within a network of functional choices. The choice a writer makes can be seen against the background of relations of contrast and dependence between one choice and another. The pluralist therefore has a theory of language which considers style in terms of the functions of language as a piece of text can be multifunctional. The pluralists approach style from the perspective of 'foregrounding' and 'deautomatisation' and they adopted more objective and convincing analysis of style and literary appreciation.

Methodology

The data for this study, which constitutes selected poems from the collection of Ojaide's Poetry, *The Eagle's Vision* were selected through the purposive sampling technique. The poems were selected based on their thematic preoccupations. Four poems were selected from this collection—"The Evidence of Hyena", "Cosmic Dirge", "Mournful Song" and "A Matter of Desires". The research was both qualitative and descriptive, the purposive sampling method was used for the selection of the data for the study and the tenets of sociolinguistics and stylistics were adopted for the analysis of the data.

Data Analysis

The analysis of the selected poems will take two dimension firstly, the data will be considered from the sociolinguistic perspective and secondly from the stylistic point of view. The sociolinguistic section of the paper addresses some contemporary social challenges that are faced by most developing nations or the third world, especially Nigeria. The social issues as addressed by the poet in the selected works are mainly on bad governance, abuse of power, and lack of justice. For instance, in "The Evidence of the Hyena", Ojaide addresses the perennial problem of oppression not only in the Niger-Delta but also in Nigeria as a whole. He is particularly worried about the degree of impunity with which people are oppressed on a daily basis without any form check by any institution or individual. He states thus:

see the leopard

flashing his teeth

atop his victim's bones;

Although, hyena is the only animal mentioned in the title of the poem, the poet decides to mention leopard as a way of indicating a general and similar pattern of oppression of the poor by the influential people. The poet is not just concerned about the oppression, but also with the show of pride and contentment of the oppressors. To further show that the trend cuts across regional barriers, cultural identities, ethnic groupings, etc. The lines of the poem read thus:

see the hyena

gamboling recklessly

atop his fat loot;

It could also be argued that Ojaide looks beyond the socio-political landscape and its antecedent challenges in the poem as he addresses some seemingly 'covert' spiritual and psychological expression by some "men of God". The mentioning of the Romans in connection with the death of Jesus is very significant to the present religious oppression on our land today. The poet apparently dislikes the idea of depriving people their right in the name religion, as is the common practice today. This is metaphorically captured in how the poet describes records manipulation, distortion, and others as a means through which different religious bodies insult our intelligence. In the poem, "The Evidence of Hyena", Ojaide successfully connects record manipulation with the problem of injustice in Nigeria. As he puts it,

> we know
>
> how they plant evidence
>
> to incriminate the innocent ones,
>
> who suffer the untold misery
>
> for what they never did…

In the poem, "Cosmic Dirge", the poets seems to be principally concerned with the need for unity, peaceful co-existence and a prosperous society where everybody will be free and happy. He cleverly revisits the Biafra war in Nigeria, during which thousands of people died over matters that were eventually resolved across the round table. The poet challenges Nigerians who are patriotic to look for people of like minds in ensuring that there is peaceful co-existence among all the ethnic groups in Nigeria. To be successful in his task, the poets reminds Nigerians of some memories that are not worthy of keeping about the experiences of many Nigerians during the Biafra war. The poets, hinges his call for peaceful coexistence on the agony of the Biafra war. He appeals to the sensitivity of the Nigerian people through a socio-historical exploration of the past and their associated effect on today as well as tomorrow. The poet makes a passionate appeal to the people to eschew violence and destruction of lives and properties. He warns people to desist from taking actions that will be regretted later. The poet contends thus:

> Before the separation,
>
> Before the final bath, a downpour
>
> of Lover's blood, neighbour's blood
>
> see the faces whose memories
>
> you'll have to keep
>
> in your heart.

The socio-historic significance of the above lines is connected with the eventual settlement of the differences between the Nigerian government on one hand, and the Bifran warlords on the other. For every matter that could be settled through dialogue, vices such as hatred, violence, destruction, killing of innocents, and others must be avoided at all costs.

A Stylistic Appraisal of Selected Poems in *The Eagle's Vision*

Stylistically, the selected poems are characterised with preponderance of striking linguistic features at the lexical, syntactic, semantic and graphological levels. Lexically, there are marked instances of allusion, word classes, repetitions, polyptotons, etc. The instances of lexical deviation cut across the selected poems under investigation.

Lexical Allusion

Allusion is a form of reference made to specific entities, to create a mental picture that presents the authorial intentions in the minds of the readers. Illustrations of allusion in the poems are cited thus:

> To this day
>
> the Romans insult our intelligence—
>
> their Governor washed off his hands

and the **Jews killed Jesus**   "The Evidence of Hyena"

Divisions threw us into deadly war—

we have never since birth been free of blood.

O **Eritrea, Anyanya, Biafra** and **Uganda!**....

Broken the myth of Ethiopia.Menelik's heritage....

Across the **Nile** snaked vertically. Once...

a separation set **black Arab** against eachother....   "Mournful Song"

The illustrations drawn from the lines of the poems reflect biblical and historical allusions. The biblical and historical evidences are used by the poet not only to create mental images in the minds of the readers but also to solidify the poet's claims of satirising the oppression of the less privilege in the society, "the innocent one*s*"

Word Class/Lexical Repetitions

The poet makes use of specific word classes that are of stylistic significances in the text such as adverbs and nouns.

>...see the hyena
>
>gamboling**recklessly**
>
>atop his fat loot;
>
>with monopoly of **whitewash**
>
>they rub out eyewitness memory
>
>and re-make the story
>
>**slantingly**

"The Evidence of Hyena"

...And they laugh, hyenas, for possessing an arcane knowledge

believing that since we are of same stock

as sold them **birthrights**, we would also dispossess ourselves

if they overturned **tipperloads** of bread before our hungry eyes

"A Matter of Desires"

The illustrations in bold represent lexical deviations at the level of word class, especially deviations in the use of adverbs and nouns. Adverbs of manner as well as compound nouns are emphasised in the illustrations as the deviants. The choice of adverbs of manner are meant to mock the rulers' injustice on the ruled, those words are not mere descriptions of events. Similarly, the use of compound nouns *tipperloads* and *birthrights*, vividly reflect the sociolinguistic background of the poet, these are evidences of the Nigerianism in the poet's linguistic choices. Other lexical deviations include the repetition of words such as;

>**Let's** swathe
>
>**Let** the death which haunts us....
>
>how is your **faith** now, that your partner is such a vulture?
>
>they would have lost their **faith**

before the final bath, a downpour of lovers' **blood**, neighbours blood "Cosmic Dirge"

Lexical repetitions are used for emphatic purposes in the poems.

Polyptotone

This simply refers to the repetition of words from the same root. There is preponderance of polyptoton in the selected poems under study.

>...over sacrificial **heads**;
>
>the butchers stir the fire....
>
>look over your **head**
>
>and not too far **ahead**   "Cosmic Dirge"
>
>...vomiting every known **misery** on the land that only knew laughter
>
>we are energised to break the jinx of failure
>
>that has up till now condemned us to a **miserable** race
>
>"A Matter of Desires"

Unlike other kinds of repetitions, polyptoton is used by the poet to achieve linguistic variations in the poem. Syntactic deviations are also evident in the data. the most prominent of which are structural repetitions which run through the selected poems.

Structural Repetitions

>**See the leopard**
>
>flashing his teeth
>
>**atop his victim's bones;**
>
>**see the hyena**
>
>gamboling recklessly
>
>**atop his fat loot;**
>
>**see the brute**

drunk with the blood

of his latest murder....

"The Evidence of Hyena"

Apart from the structural repetitions illustrated above, "the Cosmic Dirge", the sentence, *see the faces whose memories was* repeated in the first and last stanzas of the poem. Other instances of structural parallelism in the poems are:

The mountain shakes

A storm will erupt

Over sacrificial heads;

The butcher stir the fire...

Similarly, structural parallelism runs through the first and the last stanzas of the poem, "A Matter of Desire"; "fulfill the desires of their kind— fowl with corn...." These lines are repeated for the purpose of emphasis, to achieve linguistic variation and for creating analogies. Beside structural parallelism, there are preponderant cases of lexical relations such as collocates, synonymy, holonymy and hyponymy.

Synonyms: loot, bones and murder;

lovers' blood and neighbours blood

kinship and oneness

oaths and declarations of faith

separation and final bath, etc.

"The Evidence of Hyena" & "Cosmic Dirge"

jinx of failure and misery

offer and charity

war and blood, etc.

"Mournful Song" and "A Matter of Desire"

Antonyms: land and bush, love and separation

black and Arab, stagnations and revolutions

laughter and misery

hungary eyes and patient eyes

sprout and fruit, etc.

"Mournful Song" and "A Matter of Desire"

Hyponyms: teeth, bone, blood, hand, body

Arms, faces, body, hearts, head blood

Path, forest, stones

Meronyms: leopard, hyena, brute

Fowl, goat, duck, hyena, etc.

The lexical creations are used for creating imageries in the minds of the readers. They are words of strong lexical qualities which serve as means of achieving linguistic variations. Most of the lexical relations, especially antonyms and synonyms are context bound understanding the sense they convey in isolation may be difficult for the readers.

Discussions

The analysis of the selected poems under investigation from the sociolinguistic perspective has revealed that there exits crises which trend cuts across regional barriers, cultural identities, ethnic groupings which the poet bitterly decries through the lines of the poems. The poet exposes the social vices through the use of allusion, imagery, etc. The poet does not only do this, as an agent of change, he calls for change through his writings, especially through the deployment of specific linguistic features such as structural parallelism,specific tropes and schemes such as personification, simile, metaphor, and so on. The poet makes a passionate appeal to the people to eschew violence and destruction of lives and properties.

Conclusion

This study has examined selected poems of Tanure Ojaide in his collection, *The Eagle's Vision* from a socio-stylistic point of view. From the analysis done so far, it has been discovered that the author's style of writing simply depicts his historical, economic and socio-political experiences. The author has employed some elements of language in order to enable the readers deduce the poetic intentions. The use of sociolinguistics and stylistics as the frameworks for the analysis of the selected poems has unravel the misery that are inherent in the lines of the poems.

Work Cited

Carter, Ronald. "Issues in Pedagogical Stylistics: A Coda", *Language and Literature*, 2010 19 (1) 115-122.

Catano, James V. *Language, history and style*. London: Routledge, 1998

Collier, Jane M. "Researching Cultural Identity: Reconciling Interpretive and Postcolonial Perspectives". *Communication and Identity Across Cultures International and Intercultural Communication Annual*, 2008, 21, pp. 122-147

Collier, Jane M. "Cultural Identity Theory in Cultural Communication, Intercultural Communication". https://www.communicationtheory.org/cultural-identity-theory/ Accessed 28th Apr. 2018,

Collier, Jane M. and Thomas, M. "Cultural identity: An Interpretive Perspective". *Theories in Intercultural Communication: International and Intercultural Communication Annual*, 2009, 12, 99-120

Enkvist, Nils. E., John Spencer, and Michael J. Gregory, *An Approach to the Study of Style*. Mouton: The Hague, 1995.

Fairclough, Norman. *Language and Power,* London: Longman, 2001.
Halliday, Machael, A. K. and Christian M.I Matthiessen, *Introduction to Functional Grammar*, London: Routledge, 2014.

Hornby, Sydney A. *Oxford Advanced Learner's Dictionary of Current English*, USA: OxfordUniversity Press, 2010.

Leech, Geoffrey and Short, Micky. *Style in Fiction: A Linguistic Introduction to English Fictional Prose*, London: Longman, 2007.

Simpson, Paul. *Stylistics: A Resource Book for Students*. Routledge: London, 2004.

Widdowson, H. G. On the Implications of Linguistics Applied, *Applied Linguistics*, 2000, 21(1), pp. 3-25.

Environmental Activism: A Quest for Parity in Tanure Ojaide's *The Tale of the Harmattan*

Edoama Frances Odoeme

Introduction

The oil-rich Niger Delta region of Nigeria has been inundated with environmental crisis since the 1960s, when oil was discovered in commercial quantity. The magnitude of the crisis in the region, has exacerbated in recent years. Piqued by the incessant ruination of the environment of his homeland and the resultant privation of the people, Tanure Ojaide, an acclaimed poet-scholar, employs his poetic art in responding to the dire situation. In his writings, he calls attention to the unjust practices taking place in the Delta and demands for a change in method and attitude of all those involved in the exploitation of the Niger Delta landscape. The writer, whose early childhood memories of the place of his birth contrasts sharply with the actualities of his adult years, devotes a great number of his poetry collections to instigating the rescue of the plundered environment and to ensuring the restoration of socio-political and environmental justice to a region embroiled in vast and complex ecological crisis.

Thus, this paper, examines the lingering question of environmental crisis in Niger Delta as highlighted in Ojaide's *The Tale of the Harmattan*. It demonstrates how the poet deploys his poetry in interrogating the mindless exploitation of the environment of the Niger Delta and the devastating impact of the environmental injustice on the lives of the people of the region. Replete with poetic tales of degradation of the land, deprivations and impoverishment of the people, the text serves to emphasize the enormity of the environmental challenges in the region. The paper argues that through the poet's use of vivid images of lived experiences in his imaginative writings, he aims at defying the skewed socio-economic and political system in Nigeria, by prompting the demand for social justice. The oral poetic devices and images which the text inheres, reverberates the poet's yearning for the cultural humanity of his native land, as in the days of old, as he employs elements of oral poetry in challenging unjustified exploitation.

Eco-Critical Encounter and Ojaide's Poetry

Ecocriticism which focuses on the examination of the relationship between humans and their natural environment, as represented in literary works, has in recent years been expanded to cover a broad range of issues related to environmental crisis. Geta Sahu explains that the transformations in social and cultural life of people and environments of the world, have also had a corresponding impact on the ways and manner, man's attitude towards the environment are represented in literary texts (24). As one of the many strata of ecocriticism, environmental justice ecocriticism examines environmental challenges and related social problems, such as safe environment, healthy populace and equitable allocation of environmental resources, as reflected in imaginative works. In other words, it addresses environmental degradation as

well as the challenges arising from inequitable distribution of environmental benefits and ills, among the different groups of people; the mistreatment of the people who depend on the ecosystem. Thus, the theory came into being in response to representations in literary texts of issues of perceived injustice and lack of fair treatment in the allotment of gains that result from the process of harnessing the resources of a given environment.

Accordingly, environmental justice ecocriticism fuses environmental concerns with social justice in order to bring to the fore what T. V. Reed describes as "the invasive, pervasive effects of corporate capitalism" (Adamson et al 151). The theory helps to explore essential relations between postcolonial implications and environmental outcomes and discourses of nationhood / "national ecopoetics" (Estok 1). It therefore, serves as a veritable critical tool for the examination of literary works on environmental crisis, especially those of writers from postcolonial societies whose main aim has been that of renegotiating the complex socio-cultural positions in which the societies are presently enmeshed. As a postcolonial writer of note, Ojaide devotes much of his creative writings to addressing eco-critical issues and challenging the biased political economy in his home country.

Hence, critics have not only noted the prevalence of the theme of environmental justice in Ojaide's poetry, they have also observed the fervor with which the poet illuminates the themes that border on the environment and related socio-political/economic concerns in his poetry. Nesther Alu and Vashti Suwa stress how sensitive Ojaide holds the subject of the Delta in his ingenious mind, as he attempts to "uncover the deleterious social order in his society" (135). They maintain that "Tanure Ojaide's distinct dissenting voice seeks to uproot the entrenched exploitative capitalist corruption that presents a starling debate on the political maladministration, deprivation and oppression of the minority ... tribes of the Delta" (137). Philip Aghoghovwia also notes how the poet frowns upon the socio-economic imbalance taking place in Niger Delta, in his writings. Charles Bodunde likewise, observes how Ojaide weaves the Delta landscape into his art such that the visible physical disintegration of the landscape and the deteriorating social life of the people correlate (195). Uzoechi Nwagbara also asserts that in his enduring devotion to cataloguing the plights of the minority groups in a nation where socio-economic emergency abound that Ojaide has endeavored to foster a poetic sensibility that defies the horrors of the times (92). In further affirming Ojaide's fervency in the handling of environmental justice topics in his poetry Tijan Sallah declares that the most persistent and unifying theme in most of Ojaide's works "is a single-minded detestation of tyrants combined with obsessive commitment to social justice (20).

Born and raised in one of the pristine communities in the Niger Delta, Tanure Ojaide has remained fond of the region which provided him all the basic knowledge of nature and its significance to human life and existence. As evidenced in many of his writings, the poet underlines the import of his childhood experiences with the environment of his place of birth, on his life and career. His constant juxtaposition of his childhood memories with his present-day experiences speaks of the marked but undesirable changes that have taken place in the Delta since his childhood days. The poet readily attests to the adverse transformation of his "home ground" in his literary texts, in his efforts to record "the beauty and bounty of the Delta before this ill willed development took place" (Alu and Suwa 135). He affirms this, in one of his critical writings when he says:

To me as a poet, childhood is vital, because it is the repository of memory. That is why the Delta area has been so important to me ... My Delta years have become the touchstone with which to measure the rest of my life. The streams, the fauna, and the flora are symbols I continually tap... (*Poetic Imagination* 122).

Thus, Ojaide's inability to reconcile the grim and bleak atmosphere of his homeland, at present, with the peaceful and happy memories of his childhood, impels the use of his literary ingenuity in seeking to halt the environmental wreckage and social injustice taking place in the Delta. Hence, the poet's preoccupation with the fate of the Niger Delta landscape and that of the people of the region, in his writings. It is apparent, that it is not just the willful destruction of the physical environment of his land of birth, by the devastating exploits of multinational companies that riles the poet, the emotional and psychological trauma which the people are subjected, also peeves the writer. He rejects in totality the activities of the agents of capitalist systems which in addition to depriving the people of natural wealth, estranges them from their natural habitat and cultures. Therefore, in much of Ojaide's poetics, environmental activism which aims at upholding social justice, resonates. This gives credence to Simon Estok's observation that it is the activist intentions and impulse that give urgency to words of writers whose expressions are directed at creating heightened awareness through sustained calls for actions that are aimed at fostering far-reaching changes (89).

Eco-Activism in *The Tale of the Harmattan*

In the collection, *The Tale of the Harmattan*, Ojaide, in defiance of the entrenched capitalist system in Nigeria, challenges the continued environmental devastation and the loop-sided socio-economic arrangements, as he also demands for equity and fair play for a people that have been short-changed, for too long. Employing various images, metaphors, proverbs and folklores of his native community (Urhobo), the poet paints a vivid picture of the deteriorating landscape of his homeland. The three sections of the collection bear similar tales of the despoliation of the Niger Delta environment, economic marginalization of the people and the poet's resolve to challenge the sustained environmental injustice. The story of the effects of oil exploration on the flora and fauna of the Niger Delta; the impact of eco-degradation on life around the coastal line and in sea; and the call by the poet for a cohesive action in the demand for justice, is ingeniously articulated in the 27 poems, in this volume. In an apparent attempt at justifying why an urgent stop must be put to the crisis taking place in the Delta, Ojaide relives the details of the exploitation of the Niger Delta environment, in this book of poetry. The poet's angst is palpable as he takes readers through the agonizing experiences of a people who are physically deprived and psychologically gagged while being robbed of their God-given resources.

In "The goat song", a lengthy poem divided into three parts, for instance, Ojaide, utilizes the image of the domestic animal, "goat" which is mainly valued for its fecund qualities, to symbolize the place of the Niger Delta region, in a socio-political/economic imbalanced country. He positions himself as the symbol of the struggle for the soul of the Delta, as he renders divergent depictions of life in the Delta region and life in government circles in Abuja, the capital city.

> I sing the community's goat song
>
> Folks wear gold over tumours of hope;
>
> they are rounded into guarded prison
>
> south-south of the mountain palace
>
> where the king and his consorts carouse;
>
> a bacchanalia that breaks the rock of reason.
>
> The capital is so afflicted with flatulence,
>
> only thunder can halt insatiable hands
>
> from clearing the commonwealth's table
>
> of cornucopia into paunches of the lords.
>
> Those sitting on wealth are rickety, groveling
>
> on sand; globules of anguish their only share
>
> And who cares if foreigners found deep
>
> under their bare feet divine gifts of pools
>
> and started to tap the earth's underbelly
>
> for fuel to blaze brushes of progress? (*The Tale* 10).

There is an ironical twist in which the system condemns the people who are supposed to be "sitting on wealth" to penury while unfettered access to "the commonwealth" is allotted to treacherous "king and his cohorts" (*The Tale* 10/11z). Themes of corruption and avarice echo here as in many of Ojaide's collections. The selfish and morally bankrupt government officials, who blatantly display their wasteful and lavish lifestyle are only too glad to provide cover for the multinationals, that wreak havoc on the land while destroying the people's "brushes of progress" (*The Tale* 10). This affirms Ilaria Bereta's claim that environmental injustice manifests through instances of unreasonable inequality and lack of fair treatment of marginalized or disadvantaged people and social groups (1). Ojaide decries this aberrant disparity and unjust manner of distribution of the nation's resources, especially against the people whose environment has been ravaged in the process of its extraction. In addition to conjuring up thunder to strike looters, in his position as the chief priest of the

Delta, the poet's deployment of idioms such as "wear gold over tumours of hope" / "rounded into guarded prison", "rickety" / "groveling on sand" / "globules of anguish" (*The Tale* 10), to refer to the populace of the Delta region; and idioms like "king and his consorts" / "a bacchanalia", "afflicted with flatulence", "paunches of the lords" (*The Tale* 10), in describing the government officials and their deportment serves as an indication of an attempt by the poet to sensitize people to the need to counter this socio-political imbalance.

Detailing the ills of environmental exploitation on the populace, the poet sustains the tale of a people whose means of sustenance are destroyed, and their wellbeing completely disregarded, in the second part of the poem. "All along the wells brought forth rusty colouration" / "water wells exposed" (*The Tale* 10), cannot remain the same again. The poet then wonders, what the likelihood of the people's survival is, if their means of sustenance, as exemplified in "water' which is one of the basic essential elements needed for the sustenance all forms of life is sullied? How can the people ever savor the wealth of their land or "is health not the greatest wealth?" (*The Tale* 11). According to the poet, the people suffer but continue "to wear smiles over deep wounds" " (*The Tale* 10), as their wealth continue to be plundered by those who care for nothing about their wellbeing. And as the people's advocate, the poet steps in, he is up in arms against the agents of social and economic strangulation, with his song. In addition to brandishing his verbal arsenal, in the final part of the poem, Ojaide calls for the gathering of all the land "warriors" (*The Tale* 12). To boost confidence for sustained agitations against socio-economic injustice in the Niger Delta, where "the blackened stream" or "the ancestral blood" is "tapped away by giant pipes into ships / to rejuvenate foreign cities, invigorate markets; / distant places lit with wonders" while back home in the Delta, there is a total "blackout" (*Tale* 11). Ojaide taps into the African belief in "life after death" (*The Tale* 11). He assures the people of the support of the departed ones, thus upholding the customary African belief in the continued interest of the dead in the welfare of the living. He invokes the legendary folk heroes of the Delta – "Ozidi and Ogidigbo" – who are believed to detest unjust practices; and the spirits of nationalists and freedom fighters; "Mowoe and Saro-Wiwa", acclaimed warriors of their time; to join forces with the land's warriors in a bid to wrest their land from "government and the coalition of global lords" who "have snatched away" the sacred gifts of their "ancestors" (12). This ratifies Alu and Suwa's observation that Ojaide in order to mobilize heroes to action, always invokes traditional and cultural spirits who have had outstanding victories (142).

In "Priests, converts and gods", the poet bemoans the psychological rigor which ensues from the imposition of strange cultural norms. To him, this results in the alienation of the people from their original culture culminating in the disregard for the beliefs and rules that govern the use of their natural habitat. He seems greatly disturbed about the consequences of abandoning one's core cultural values which he says equals the effacement of one's self-worth. By this, Ojaide validates Frantz Fanon's assertion that one who allows inferiority complex to sprout in his/her soul is courting "the death and burial of its cultural originality" (18). Ojaide relays:

Pentecostal converts burnt down the primeval grove –

there, they believed, witches metamorphosed into owls;

they did not even know what animals they had become,

when they were *born again*, living in self-renunciation (*Tale* 13).

The poet reveals how the imperialists have gone from tearing "down the forest that covered" the people "with green foliage" and trashing "the natural canopies" under the pretext of providing modern infrastructural facilities, to causing mental disequilibrium in the minds of people who are already afflicted with economic woes and health hazards. This is done to further subdue the people and to gain total control over them and their land. The unsuspecting populace's woes are doubled when in "worshipping the foreign-accented god, they thrust a blazing firebrand / at the behind of the war-god who fled his guard without looking back" (*The Tale* 13), leaving the dispirited folks exposed to more dangers. The poet resents this attempt to destroy the mystical affinity between the people and their spiritual benefactors and calls for a stop to this anomaly.

Furthermore, Ojaide uses metaphorical representation of the distasteful tale of the political divide in Nigeria, to provoke the national question, interrogating the waning nationalist ethos and the increasing ethnic divide, using the images such as "devouring plant" from "up North" and "campfires" in the "South".

Up North the Sahara devouring plants advances ferociously

after gulping the River Niger in a generation -long fit of thirst.

In the South the campfires of oil barons litter the landscape;

stoked all year round by helmet-wearing graduates

who consider themselves lucky, paid foreign currency

instead of naira; an astute ploy to buy their loyalty…

We know of capital gain from the blessed but besieged land

will go down the drain for a caste to maintain its smug smile.

The priests that came from abroad warned of the inferno

that would consume those who did not heed their commandments –

they were wrong in attributing hell to another life; it is

here victims already suffer daily pangs from profiteers,

condemned to burning winds of gas flares and streams

of boiling oil combustible they burn all in their wake (*The Tale* 13/14).

The poet is peeved by unpatriotic activities of the ruling class. They do not only engage in nepotistic acts but also collaborate with foreigner plunderers to marginalize the people of the Niger Delta region, upsetting their cultural values, in the process. He cautions the people to be mindful of the devious tactics of the exploiters who devise manifold ploys in their bid to continue oppressing the people. Living in the Niger Delta at present, for him, is synonymous with living in hell, if not more horrendous. Therefore, the threat of some suffering in the afterlife for refusal to remain subservient, is a ruse and should be ignored. The "astute ploy to buy their loyalty" with "paid foreign currency instead of naira" should also be recognized for what it is, a strategy to impose the "divide and rule" policy of the capitalists which negates the communal camaraderie. The poet is advocating against docile conducts while encouraging spirited actions from the populace, for a chance to redeem themselves from their oppressors.

In "Quatrain suite" Ojaide, in a manner characteristic of a cantor in an oral poetic performance, renders his poetic divination in lyrical quatrain verses. With the use of flashback, the poet juxtaposes the Delta landscape before and after oil exploration, as he laments the turn of events.

The map of my homeland has changed.

The cartographers blot out forest and rivers.

Oil wells and flares dot the new landscape –

now nobody recognizes the beauty queen's face…

for good luck I carry about memories of floodwater…

in gurgling streams and creeks, the entire land a seascape

when my bait-free new hooks caught catfish and mudfish…

Evergreen bald, every head bowed in disgrace.

No season grows backs flared or suffocated leaves

And the circle of self-succeeding generations dies.

Green is now scarce commodity in the rain forest. (*The Tale* 18/19).

The poet's deployment of imagery clearly designates the marked contrast between the Niger Delta's bioregion of "then" and "now" which shows the harm that has befallen the "evergreen" environment where "forests and rivers" have been blotted out and only "oil wells and flares dot the new landscape", rendering "the beauty queen's face" (*Tale* 18) unrecognizable.

For this reason, Ojaide is confounded by the inaction of the international communities to the violent desecration of the Delta region. Reproaching the concept of globalization which the poet believes to be a hoax, he muses on the connivance of the purported globalists, in the blatant abuse of his homeland.

The eye of the earth beholds a vandalized fortune.

The ears of the earth numb from the deep silence.

Its veins clogged by an abundance of oily grease,

its heart beats an irregular drum that fades away.

The iroko knows not how it can survive the iron era…

Globalization is a category-5 hurricane; its direction

escapes forecast – it leaves litters in an insane trail (*The Tale* 19/20).

The poet reappraises the unquantifiable loss suffered by the people of the region and the capital gain accruable to the violators, in the process.

> The rich among us used to boast of the many barrels
>
> of palm oil they produced in the season of industry.
>
> Then came spills and flares that burnt palm trees.
>
> Today government and Shell toast their oil fortune.
>
> The birds and beetles lost their refuge, as people
>
> of the creeks lost their sun, moon, and stars to fumes.
>
> Why are survivors of globalization assault only
>
> the insignia of commanders-in-chief, vulture and cobras? (*The* 20).

The crumbling social and economic mainstay of the people is perpetuated by the country's fraudulent government officials and Shell, the symbol of the manipulative multinational firms, who ironically are also the beneficiaries of the Delta misfortune. One would have expected a turn of events in the democratic era, but the poet laments how the populace unfortunately still "bleed" in this new dispensation, under the yoke of misrepresentation.

Therefore, in this verse, the poet gives vent to the paradox of the disreputable globalization process. To him, it is advantageous to only certain groups and not the poor masses who are being driven out of "the native soil" to strange and unfriendly abodes – land "where nobody lives" (*The Tale* 20). He regrets the fact that when these sojourners eventually return to their native land, they can hardly differentiate "their home from others in the wilted dominion" (*The Tale* 20).

Thus, in aligning the postcolonial ambiguities with environmental crisis, Ojaide highlights the hydra-headed challenges confronting the postcolonial societies and its citizens. This brings to mind Ojaide's own thesis which he captures in one of his collections, that for members of marginalized groups, especially citizens of postcolonial nations, "it no longer matters where one lives", because the original homeland which in most cases, is ravaged by multinationals is as inhabitable as any foreign location which is always replete with peculiar strangeness for the emigrant.

The poem, "For my grandchild" encapsulates the bleak future of a region blessed with abundant resources but which perishes from want of material goods and life opportunities. Danger looms in the region because there are no prospects for the youths' development and empowerment in situations where the children who "have had no scholarships ... can't fish or tap rubber" as the poet once did because the river has been "transformed into a snake of a tomb / and the forest fraught with flares and fumes" (*The Tale* 23). And all that the government of the day does is to make empty promises. With the use of the African oral technique of story-telling, Ojaide depicts the picture of dejection, deploying images of slavery and repression to portray hapless condition of the indigenes of the ravaged Delta region.

> With crude oil gushing into slave ships
>
> refurbished as free-market super-tankers...
>
> No jobs for the graduates in the oil sector
>
> even as wells litter the family's farmlands.
>
> In the daily dearth of prospects staring at all,
>
> mobile policemen brandish guns in the sun
>
> and from a safe distance above the ground,
>
> hired retired marines keep the pipelines safe.
>
> Villages of imploring eyes marching, hands up-
>
> raised with green-leafed branches, mowed down.
>
> CNN & BBC embedded with Chevron and Shell
>
> Report that local women, stripping before cameras
>
> to save their dying children and men, are primitive.
>
> In their secure wings they know not Ogoni's agonies...
>
> with refill slave ships refurbished as super-tankers
>
> anchored ... and poaching inland as centuries ago (*Tale* 23).

The poem is packed with metaphors of brutalization and subjugation (images of policemen brandishing guns, retired marines keeping watch, people engaging in peaceful protest being mowed down), used by the poet to express socio-political domination of his people. The economic conquest and enslavement, reminiscent of the Trans-Atlantic Slave Trade, are perpetuated in connivance with world super brands and big media outfits. These nefarious activities against the people, which are ironically sponsored by the proceeds from the oil wells of the Niger Delta, are disguised as free and mutual trade deals. The vivid portrayal of the dire situation in the region by the poet serves as an urgent call for action in stalling the complete destruction of the environment and an impending annihilation of the masses of the Delta. Charles Bodunde notes how Ojaide through his choice of words in most of his creative pieces, urges readers to "condemn the political and economic agenda, which erodes the normal bond between landscape and man" (206).

Just like in the last poem, Ojaide's succinctly expresses his aversion to what he considers to be the exploitation and commodification of the Niger Delta region by capitalists, in "Market day". The manipulative trade deals, according to him, are favorable only to the multinationals and their coconspirators. These devious merchants ransack the rich Delta region, carting away precious goods and products without due recompense, to the owners of the land. Imploring one of the numerous benevolent traditional gods of the region, the god of commerce, in a manner akin to that of a traditional priest, the poet pleads with the god for assistance in wresting their land from looters and restoring the glory of the region.

> O market god, conjurer god of the milling place,
>
> god of colours, god of flavours and the handmade,
>
> fill the market with the items that tales passed to us
>
> but we now find beyond our means in distant places...
>
> Welcome strangers as always – they enrich us –
>
> but take out poachers, arsonists, and robbers;
>
> bring back our produce and products of our hands;
>
> fill our sheds with what stories credit you with pride (*Tale* 26/27).

For the poet, the atrocious economic marginalization has gone on for too long in his homeland, and he is desirous of an urgent positive change. As a firm believer in the traditional practices of his people, Ojaide is confident that if the people fortify their ranks; continue to maintain their close affinity with the land's many deities, as in the days of old; that in no time, the land will be freed and the people will be able to enjoy the wealth of their land again and will sing "the song of abundance" (*The Tale* 27).

As illustrated in the collection, the burden of the ecological damage to the Niger Delta environment has assumed a monumental proportion, and in "At the kaima bridge", Ojaide continues to recount the adverse effect the activities of the neo-imperialists have had on the entire biotic life of the region. The ecosystem has been seriously degraded, and from the images deployed by the poet, the loss is colossal – with forests and aquatic lives extremely depleted. But above all of these, it seems that what is most irksome to the poet is the cultural disruption and the alienation of the people from the land of their birth, that this environmental crisis has engendered. The poet relays:

I have not seen a regatta in three decades.

Nor have I seen the island's boat of songs

raise a ritual paddle in salute to high gods

that astronauts now suffocate with satellites…

Neighbours are surrendering their homes

to destruction by the fires from above.

Others have the soil burning underfoot,

their shield of green gone; mere ashes.

The refuges are removed from the fields

in company buses, a humanitarian gesture;

then in diarrhoea-infected camps force-fed

genetically modified corn meant for cows (*Tale* 34/35).

Casting his mind back, the poet recalls attempts made in the past to reclaim the lost land but maintains that the "resistance army" formed to declare "sovereignty" over the resources were not formidable enough to push "back the poachers". Therefore, he charges the masses to defy the brutality of the exploiters, come out again, this time in full force, to demand for what is rightfully theirs.

Do I want to shed blood defending the wealth

that the gods themselves have given up…

Is revolution dead and must the Egbesu boys

surrender rights of ownership and humanity

to the brigand lord and his fierce livery

of insatiable appetites raising a flaming flag? (*Tale* 35).

If the land has to be rescued from hands of the swindlers, and the people's means of livelihood restored, the people must revive the struggle. With the employment of rhetorical questions, the people's advocate, Ojaide, exhorts the people's army to stand up to the challenge. Through the poet's use of the metaphor of the "wobbling Kaima Bridge and the images of "oil-soaked water spirits" (*The Tale* 35), and the absence of fishermen, boat regatta and swimmers in the Delta rivers, his activist's intent becomes unmistakable, in the last verse of the poem.

In "For the egbesu boys" Ojaide who seems unable to continue to condone the hapless destruction of the Delta bio-region and the impoverishment of the people, unreservedly summons the faithful followers of the Ijaw god of warfare, "the egbesu boys" to lead the battle for the restoration of the Niger Delta environment. Like their god, Egbesu, who fights a just cause, the poet affirms using idiomatic expressions (derived from the rich repertoire of the oral poetic forms) of the virtuousness of the battle:

Who breaks into your home to kill you

draws from you all means of self-defence

who trespasses into your inherited land

draws the wrath of your ancestor and gods...

Who comes to your home to rape your bride

tests your courage before the vile act ... (*The* 42).

The poet also assures the fighters of victory because he, as a "devotee of Ivwri", a colleague of their god, has invoked the "warrior spirits".

With your white headband the god you serve

recognizes your steadfast faith in his power –

Egbesu retreats not from a war thrusts upon him!

Supreme warrior, Egbesu runs not from a fight...

> I call on you, Egbesu, marshal of the mangroves,
>
> acclaimed war-god of born fishers and farmers,
>
> to stand steadfast behind your great boys…
>
> I, devotee of Ivwri, colleague of your Ifri, sing this.
>
> Egbesu, I invoke your warrior spirit for the boys…
>
> Egbesu boys, dismiss with your blood the charge
>
> of robbery by the coalition of global powers (*The Tale* 42/43).

The images of invincibility and conquest as woven around the people's army and as denoted by the inability of the "Navy" to "penetrate the fingers of the Niger" signifies hope for the eventual emancipation of the beleaguered Delta environment.

> … the poaching army will stop by the waterside;
>
> the Navy cannot penetrate the fingers of the Niger
>
> and those who know their land from birth
>
> cannot be pushed out by armed invaders…
>
> history is replete with withdrawing troops
>
> of occupiers; shame and death await them…
>
> true devotees, you have shown deep faith
>
> and Egbesu arms you with an arsenal of justice…
>
> Justice is invincible and robbers will be routed… (*The Tale* 44).

The poet's optimism as expressed in the last part of the poem aims at assuaging the pains of the masses and inspiring them to boldly face the future while demanding for their rights.

Ojaide, in "Mass hunt", employs the allegorical phrases from the oral source, in the expression of his revolutionary enthusiastic message aimed at spurring the people on to mass action.

> Let's drive them into their holes:
>
> ants that condemn our feet for murder
>
> locusts that consume our greens
>
> crickets that perforate our pots
>
> rats that bite our soles in deep sleep
>
> fowls that ambush us with droppings…
>
> and what bigger holes will be left
>
> to swallow survivors of the mass hunt (*The Tale* 59).

With this poem, Ojaide reaffirms his poetic mission of using his art to restore hope to the hopeless masses that are plagued by an unjust system. He demonstrates his firm devotion to this vision of social responsibility.

Conclusion

Although Ojaide's desire for positive change for his home environment runs through many of his poetry collections, in *The Tale of the Harmattan*, his unwavering commitment to liberating his homeland from the shackles of capitalism is heightened. His dedication to the cause of resisting injustice and ensuring equity for the homeland is brought to the fore, in the text. The consciousness of the social responsibility which he strives to bring to bear on his place of birth, runs through the poems in this collection. The poet is well aware of fact that attaining the desired goal of liberating his desecrated land, restoring fairness and ensuring parity for the sidelined citizens of the Niger Delta region, could only be achieved through a sustained struggle. This prompts the ingenious deployment of words and images as weapons of warfare in his attempts at awakening the people to their individual and collective obligations. Stressing Ojaide's devotion to the cause of the environment and the well-being of the people of the Niger Delta, Bodunde remarks that even the deployment of images in Ojaide's poetry serves to sensitize the people of the importance of collective action and human rights struggle in rescuing their degraded environment and ensuring justice (196).

Thus, conscious of his role as both a poet and a priest, Ojaide deploys the poems in this collection (which are imbued with oral poetic elements), as verbal weaponry to demand for fair treatment of the people and the environment of the Niger Delta, and to implore his fellow citizens of the region to join forces in ensuring the institution of just and unbiased practices.

Accordingly, the poet mediates resistance against ecological devastation, injustice and cultural disorientation, in this book of poetry. Having lost confidence in the political representation in the country, he enlists the services of the people's army. Using his linguistic ammunitions, he propels the people to action while fortifying them with the spirits of the ancestors and past heroes, the custodians of the original cultures. The poet's adept blend of the oral poetic devices in his writings is indicative of his rootedness in the cultural practices of his people, a norm which he wants upheld at all times, because for him, the cultural beliefs and the physical environment are interwoven.

Works Cited

Aghoghovwia, Philip Onoriode. "Versifying the Environment and the Oil Encounter: Tanure Ojaide's Delta Blues & Home Songs". *Alternation*, vol.6 2013, pp 175-196. Accessed 8 April 2015.

Alu, Nesther, Suwa Vashti Yusuf. "Tanure Ojaide: The Poet-Priest of the Niger-Delta and the Land Saga". *An International Journal of Language, Literature and Gender Studies*, 1.1 (2012): 132-144.

Bareta, Ilaria. "Some Highlights on the Concept of Environmental Justice and its Use". Journals.openedition.org. Accessed 12 March 2018.

Bodunde, Charles. "Tanure Ojaide's Poetry and the Delta Landscape: A study of Delta Blues and Home Songs. *Writing the Homeland: The Poetry and Politics of Tanure Ojaide. Bayreuth African Studies*, edited by Onookome Okome, vol. 60, pp 195-208. Accessed 16 August 2016.

Estok, Simon. "Discourses of Nation, National Ecopoetics, and Ecocriticism in the Face of the US: Canada and Korea as Case Studies". *Comparative American Studies*, vol. 7 no. .2, 2009, pp 85-97. Accessed 11 March 2018.

Fanon, Frantz. *The Wretched of the Earth*. Translated by Richard Philcox. New York: Grove Press, 2004.

Nwagbara, Uzoechi. "In the Shadow of the Imperialists: A Philosophico-Materialist Reading of Tanure Ojaide's *Delta Blues & Home Songs* and *Daydream of Ants and Other Poems*". *SKASE Journal of Literary Studies,* vol.3. no.1. 2011, pp 76-96. Accessed 20 February 2014.

Ojaide, Tanure. *Poetic Imagination in Black Africa*. Durham: Carolina Academy, 1996.

—-. *The Tale of the Harmattan*. Ibadan: Kraft Books, 2015.

Reed, T.V. "Toward an Environmental Justice Ecocriticism". *The Environmental Justice Reader: Politics, Poetics and Pedagogy* edited by Joni Adamson, Mei-Mei Evans, Rachael Stein. Arizona: UP, 2002.

Sahu, Geeta. "Ecocriticism – Understanding the Relationship between Literature and Environment in Indian English Novels". *Sai Om Journal of Arts and Education*, vol.1 no.1 2014 pp 23-26. Accessed 18 March 2018.

Sallah, Tijan. "The Eagles Vision: The poetry of Tanure Ojaide. *Research in African Litrerature,* vol.26 no.1 1999, pp 20-29. Accessed 10 February 2014.

Appendix

Citation on Professor Tanure Ojaide, NNOM,

Tanure Ojaide is a renowned scholar-poet who bestrides the academic and creative worlds like a colossus; a widely–travelled man who has successfully rendered quality services in academics and creativity to virtually all the states in Nigeria and continents of the world; a man whose life and work both attest to the fact that the quality of a man's life is measured more by the humble, selfless and impactful service to the people, a service from which one ought not to retire.

Born into the family of Dafetanure and Avwerhoke Ojaide of Okpara Inland, in Delta State of Nigeria, on April 24, 1948, as the first male child of his parents, he automatically assumes the position of a priest and by extension an oracle. Considering the temper and range of his artistic productivity, Ojaide is not just a bucolic priest and oracle, but by implication he has become a cultural priest, a social priest and a universal oracle.

Professor Tanure Ojaide had his early education at St. George's Grammar School, Obinomba, and Federal Government College, Warri. He later attended University of Ibadan where he received his Bachelor of Arts degree in English. It was at the University of Ibadan that Ojaide began writing some of the poems that appeared in his first published collection, *Children of Iroko and Other Poems*. He published in student magazines such as *The Beacon* and *Pelican*. After graduating in 1971, Ojaide worked briefly at the Federal Ministry of Education, Lagos. He moved to a teaching job at St. Kelvin's Grammar School, Kokori, a few kilometers from his birth-place, and was later relocated to Federal Government College, Warri. He remains the first former student of the College to return there after acquiring higher education. After teaching for two years in the newly established Petroleum Training Institute, Effurun, for two years (1975-1977), he went to teach at the University of Maiduguri in 1977. The University of Maiduguri in 1978 sent him to the United States to pursue graduate studies at the Syracuse University where he earned the Master of Arts in Creative Writing and a Doctorate. in English. He returned to the Department of English at Maiduguri on December 18, 1981. He remained there for nine years, teaching and writing. In 1990, Ojaide accepted a sabbatical leave offer at Whitman College, Walla Walla, Washington, where he held the Visiting Johnston Professor for that year. After completing the sabbatical year at Walla Walla, he took a tenure track job at the Department of African and African American Studies, University of North Carolina, United States of America. He is currently a Full Professor of Africana Studies at that University. He has equally been appointed the Frank Porter Graham Distinguished Professor of Africana Studies since 2006.

Ojaide is arguably Africa's most prolific poet. He is also a scholar, nationalist, Pan-Africanist, short story writer, essayist, teacher, and novelist. He has published 20 collections of poetry, 3 memoirs, 3 collections of short stories, 4 novels, about a hundred articles in international indexed journals and books across the world, and 7 scholarly books on African Literature, including *Poetic Imagination in Black Africa* (1996), *Poetry, Performance, and Art: Udje Dance Songs of the Urhobo People* (2003), *Contemporary African Literature: New Approaches* (2012), *Indigeniety, Globalization, and African Literature* (2015), and *Culture and Literature in Global Africa* (2018).

Tanure Ojaide is not just another writer on the long assembly line. His imaginative art and scholarship have earned him numerous awards across the world. A Fellow in Writing of the University of Iowa, his poetry awards include the Commonwealth Poetry Prize for the Africa Region (1987), the All-Africa Okigbo Prize for Poetry (1988, 1997), the BBC Arts and Africa Poetry Award (1988), and the Association of Nigerian Authors Poetry Award (1988, 1994, 2003, and 2011). His first novel, *Sovereign Body*, was a runner-up for The Commonwealth Literature Prize for the Africa Region in 2005. His non-fiction, *Drawing the Map of Heaven: An African Writer's Experience of America*, was a runner-up for the Penguin Prize for African Writing (2010). He received a National Endowment for the Humanities Fellowship (1999/2000) to collect and study the "Udje Dance Songs of Nigeria's Urhobo People." He has twice received the Fulbright fellowship (2002/03 and 2013/14), and the Carnegie African Diaspora Fellowship (2016). He has read from his poetry in Britain, Harbourfront (Canada), International Poetry Festival, Medellin (Colombia, 2013), France, Pan-African Poetry Festival, Accra (Ghana, 2008), Israel, Malaysia, Mexico, Nigeria, Spain, World Poetry Festival, Rotterdam (The Netherlands, 1992), the United States, Poetry Africa (South Africa, 2005), and Sahitya Akademi World Poetry Festival, New Delhi (March 21-24, 2014). Three international conferences have been held at Delta State University, Abraka, Nigeria, in July 2005 and July 2008 and the University of Port Harcourt (May 2-5, 2018) respectively to discuss Ojaide's writings. Ojaide was the 2005 recipient of the University of North Carolina at Charlotte's First Citizen's Bank Scholar Award for his creative writing and scholarship and the 2016 African Literature Association Folon-Nichols Award for African Writer of Excellence. In 2016 he was awarded the Nigerian National Order of Merit for the Humanities. His poetry has been translated into Chinese, Dutch, French, German, Spanish, Sanskrit and Hindi.

The body of Ojaide's literary oeuvre is pivotal in what is today designated as the "literatures of the Niger Delta." This is a distinct body of literary expression that has stayed close to the checkered but calibrated history of the subjugation of the peoples of the Niger Delta region of Nigeria. This body of literature calls to question the history of European colonization and its aftermath, especially it regards oil exploration and exploitation. Tanure Ojaide's contribution to African poetry is intricately tied to his Urhobo and Pan-Edo origins. A strong believer in the integrity of African cultures and their meaning to the African artists in a globalized world, Ojaide appropriates modes of oral performance in his culture and then transforms them to fit into his larger poetic concerns, which are clearly visible in his very first collection of poems, *Children of Iroko and Other Poems*. While Ojaide's poetry resonates with universal human values and aspirations, the core of its meaning-making techniques is in the specificity of Urhobo oral traditions, especially the bold and highly poetic lyrics of the Udje dance songs. As a cultural entrepreneur, Ojaide transforms the "curse-poetry" of the Udje singer into a system for addressing the ills of postcolonial Nigeria. Ojaide achieves three extraordinary literary feats by this singular act of artistic transmogrification. He brings his Urhobo culture into the poetic and scholarly debates of African literary forms while at the same time calling specific attention to the social and cultural geography of the abject conditions of the Niger Delta. And above all, by not allowing the agony of the failure and weaknesses of human existence to becloud his artistic vision, Ojaide remains a very sensitive poet who celebrates the triumph of humanity over tyranny, and the enduring power of art in negotiating human existence. Interestingly, one will easily notice an intricate relationship between Ojaide's goals as a scholar and an artist. Professor Tanure Ojaide has functioned as external examiner to Universities in North America, Asia, and Africa.

   Most of his students and colleagues continue to admire Professor Ojaide for his commitment to academics, his exemplary humility and liberal attitude to life. He does not see students and mentees just as students, but as fellow humans and friends who should be treated fairly and decently at every point of interaction. Gentle and accessible, he gives a human face to his University teaching. Professor Ojaide is a man of impressive personality. Indeed, he is a "most sensible individual." In him is a fine combination of the neoclassic ideal of rationality, the profound thoughtfulness of the romantics, and the nobility of African humanity. A lively, humorous and warm-hearted man, Professor Ojaide takes people for who they are, irrespective of status, gender, class, or religion. He is completely detribalized, such that his friendship cuts across ethnic boundaries. A true scholar, his mind is untainted by prejudices, pettiness, and bigotry.

   Tanure Ojaide is total gentleman and teacher/mentor-friend. He is a rare example of the teacher-friend, an academic colossus, Africa's most prolific poet, world-renowned literary scholar, cultural enthusiast, an innovator, a foresighted and thorough-bred manager of men and materials, an ebullient Professor, Professor of Professors, Frank Porter Graham Distinguished Professor of Africana Studies, an optimistic lover of humanity, a likeable, humble, unassuming and companionable gentleman.

Notes on Contributors

Adetayo ALABI is an Associate Professor of English at the University of Mississippi (USA).

Saeedat B. ALIYU (PhD) teaches in the Department of English at Kwara State University, Malete, Nigeria.

Zaynab ANGO is of the Department of English, Federal University Dutse, Nigeria.

Okwudiri ANASIUDU is a PhD student in the Deparment of English Studies, University of Port Harcourt, Nigeria.

Psalms Emeka CHINAKA (PhD) is a Senior Lecturer in the Deparment of English Studies, University of Port Harcourt, Nigeria.

Mariam Titilope GOBIR, Department of Linguistics, African and European Languages, Kwara State University, Malete.

Obari GOMBA (PhD) teaches Literature and Creative Writing at the University of Port Harcourt, Nigeria.

Adama Haruna IDRISU, Mohammed Goni College of Legal and Islamic Studies, (An Affiliate of University of Maiduguri), Borno State, Nigeria

Honoré MISSIHOUN (PhD) is a Visiting Lecturer in the Department of Africana Studies, University of North Carolina at Charlotte, USA.

Edoama Frances ODUEME, University of Lagos, Akoka – Yaba, Lagos, Nigeria

Enajite Eseoghene OJARUEGA (PhD) is the Head of English and Literary Studies at Delta State University, Abraka, Nigeria.

Onookome OKOME (PhD) is Professor of English and Film Studies at University of Albreta, Canada.

Mathias Iroro ORHERO is of the Department of English and Literary Studies, Delta State University, Nigeria.

Daniel George UDO is of the Department of English, University of Uyo, Nigeria.

Onyemaechi UDUMUKWU is a Professor of English Studies at the University of Port Harcourt in Nigeria.

Moshood ZAKARIYAH, Department of Linguistics, African and European Languages, Kwara State University, Malete.

www.ingramcontent.com/pod-product-compliance
Lightning Source LLC
Chambersburg PA
CBHW051051230426
43666CB00012B/2647